Keeping Up
Up
with the
Quants

Keeping Up *with the* Quants

YOUR GUIDE TO UNDERSTANDING AND USING ANALYTICS

Thomas H. Davenport

Jinho Kim

Harvard Business Review Press

Boston, Massachusetts

Copyright 2013 Harvard Business School Publishing Corporation

Printed in the United States of America

10 9 8 7 6 5 4 3 2 1

Library of Congress Cataloging-in-Publication Data

Davenport, Thomas H., 1954-
  Keeping up with the quants : your guide to understanding and using analytics/ Thomas H. Davenport, Jinho Kim.
       pages cm
  Includes bibliographical references.
  ISBN 978-1-4221-8725-8 (alk. paper)
  1. Management—Mathematical models.   2. Decision making—Mathematical models.   3. Problem solving—Mathematical models.   I. Title.
  HD30.25.D366 2013
  332.63'2042—dc23

                                                        2012047012

The paper used in this publication meets the requirements of the American National Standard for Permanence of Paper for Publications and Documents in Libraries and Archives Z39.48-1992.

Contents

Acknowledgments

Tom thanks (and dedicates his portion of the book) to his loving wife of more than thirty years, Joan Powell Davenport. His sons Hayes and Chase have left the nest now, but they still support Dad's work remotely. The Harvard Business School Division of Research was less loving, but did provide useful research support.

Jinho thanks John and Bonnie Ries for their enthusiastic support and encouragement, including their proofreading of the original manuscript. Particular thanks go to Jung-Hwa Shin for motivating and consistently supporting Jinho in writing this book. Jinho also thanks his elder daughter Nuri, his son-in-law Dong-Wook, and his younger daughter Youngri for their love and inspiration. Jinho dedicates his share of this book to his mother, Tae-Hwa Cho, for her love and wisdom.

Tom and Jinho both thank Melinda Merino for great editing at Harvard Business Review Press, as well as all the other talented staff who make the Press the best business publisher in the business. Thanks, too, to Mark Allen for providing the charming illustrations. We'd also like to thank all the groundbreaking quants and quantitatively oriented executives, living or dead, who provided us with the examples in this book. We are merely the chroniclers of their heroic exploits.

Keeping Up
Up
with the
Quants

1

Why Everyone Needs Analytical Skills

We live in a world awash with data. Data is proliferating at an aston-ishing rate—we have more and more data all the time, and much of it was collected in order to improve decisions about some aspect of business, government, or society. If we can't turn that data into bet-ter decision making through quantitative analysis, we are both wast-ing data and probably creating suboptimal performance. Therefore, our goal in this book is to show you how quantitative analysis works—even if you do not have a quantitative background—and how you can use it to make better decisions.

The Rise of Analytics and Big Data

The rise of data is taking place in virtually every domain of society. If you're into sports, you undoubtedly know about *moneyball*, the transformation of professional baseball—and by now virtually every major sport—by use of player performance data and analytics. If you're into online gaming, you probably realize that every aspect of your game behavior is being collected and analyzed by such companies as Zynga and Electronic Arts. Like movies? If so, you probably know about the algorithms Netflix uses to predict what movies you will like. You may not have heard that a few producers of Hollywood movies, including Relativity Media, employ algorithms to decide which movies to back financially.

Of course, there are different types of data. Some is collected and managed for transactional purposes—for example, your company or organization keeps track of the date you started work or your vacation balance. But after a while, organizations have accumulated a lot of data and they want to make sense of it and make decisions on the basis of it. Data on human resources transactions can also be explored with analytics. Organizations might ask questions like, "How many employees are likely to retire next year?" or "Is there a relationship between using all your vacation days and your annual performance rating?"

But data and analytics don't just improve internal decision making. Many Internet-based organizations—Google, Facebook, Amazon, eBay, and others—are using so-called big data from online transactions not only to support decisions but to create new product offerings and features for customers. Whether you're seeking better internal decisions or more value for customers, that's where analytics come in—they summarize data, find the meaning in it, and find patterns in it. Making sense of and extracting value from data can

What Are Analytics?

By *analytics,* we mean the extensive use of data, statistical and quantitative analysis, explanatory and predictive models, and fact-based management to drive decisions and add value.[a]

Analytics can be classified as descriptive, predictive, or prescriptive according to their methods and purpose. *Descriptive analytics* involve gathering, organizing, tabulating, and depicting data and then describing the characteristics about what is being studied. This type of analytics was historically called *reporting*. It can be very useful, but doesn't tell you anything about why the results happened or about what might happen in the future.

Predictive analytics go beyond merely describing the characteristics of the data and the relationships among the variables (factors that can assume a range of different values); they use data from the past to predict the future. They first identify the associations among the variables and then predict the likelihood of a phenomenon—say, that a customer will respond to a particular product advertisement by purchasing it—on the basis of the identified relationships. Although the associations of variables are used for predictive purposes, we are not assuming any explicit cause-and-effect relationship in predictive analytics. In fact, the presence of causal relationships is not always necessary to make accurate predictions.

Prescriptive analytics, including methods such as experimental design and optimization, go even further. Like a prescription from a doctor, they suggest a course of action. *Experimental design* tries to answer the questions of *why* something happened by conducting experiments. To make causal inferences with confidence in causal research, researchers must manipulate one or more independent variables and effectively control other extraneous variables.

If the test group—the one with the experimental condition present—performs substantially better than the control group—then the decision maker should apply that condition broadly.

Optimization, another prescriptive technique, attempts to identify the ideal level of a particular variable in its relationship to another. For example, we might be interested in identifying the price of a product that is most likely to lead to high profitability for a product. Similarly, optimization approaches could identify the level of inventory in a warehouse that is most likely to avoid stock-outs (no product to sell) in a retail organization.

Analytics can be classified as qualitative or quantitative according to the process employed and the type of data that are collected and analyzed. *Qualitative analysis* aims to gather an in-depth understanding of the underlying reasons and motivations for a phenomenon. Usually unstructured data is collected from a small number of nonrepresentative cases and analyzed nonstatistically. Qualitative analytics are often useful tools for exploratory research—the earliest stage of analytics. *Quantitative analytics* refers to the systematic empirical investigation of phenomena via statistical, mathematical, or computational techniques. Structured data is collected from a large number of representative cases and analyzed statistically.

There are various types of analytics that serve different purposes for researchers:

- **Statistics:** The science of collection, organization, analysis, interpretation, and presentation of data

- **Forecasting:** The estimation of some variable of interest at some specified future point in time as a function of past data

- **Data mining:** The automatic or semiautomatic extraction of previously unknown, interesting patterns in large quantities of data through the use of computational algorithmic and statistical techniques

- **Text mining:** The process of deriving patterns and trends from text in a manner similar to data mining

- **Optimization:** The use of mathematical techniques to find optimal solutions with regard to some criteria while satisfying constraints

- **Experimental design:** The use of test and control groups, with random assignment of subjects or cases to each group, to elicit the cause and effect relationships in a particular outcome

Although the list presents a range of analytics approaches in common use, it is unavoidable that considerable overlaps exist in the use of techniques across the types. For example, *regression analysis,* perhaps the most common technique in predictive analytics, is a popularly used technique in statistics, forecasting, and data mining. Also, *time series analysis,* a specific statistical technique for analyzing data that varies over time, is common to both statistics and forecasting.

a. Thomas Davenport and Jeanne G. Harris, *Competing on Analytics* (Boston: Harvard Business School Press, 2007), 7.

only be done through mathematical or statistical analysis of data—in a word, *analytics* (see "What Are Analytics?")

The type of transactional data mentioned above for human resource decisions is structured (easily captured in rows and columns), quantitative, and in relatively small volumes (a terabyte or two even in large corporations). It's a traditional environment for analytics, so let's call it *small data*. It used to be the only option for analytics.

Today, however, big companies, nonprofit organizations, and small start-ups are excited about *big data*—unstructured data in large volumes. It might come from online discussions on the Internet, footage from video cameras, or DNA analysis of a group of patients in a hospital. These types of data tend to be much larger—sometimes in the multipetabyte range. For example, Google processes about 24 petabytes of Internet data per day, and AT&T transfers about 30 petabytes per day of voice and data telecommunications. Through new software and hardware technologies, we can now analyze big data and begin to unlock its meaning. (See "What Do We Mean by *Big Data*?")

What Do We Mean by *Big Data*?

The term *big data* is used to mean volumes of data that are unusually large, or types of data that are unstructured. Some examples include:

- Thirty billion pieces of content were added to Facebook this month by more than 600 million users.

- The social games company Zynga processes over 1 petabyte of game data per day.

- YouTube users watch more than 2 billion videos per day.

- Twitter users perform 32 billion searches per month.

- Google users performed almost 5 billion searches per day in 2011.

- Over 2.5 billion text messages were sent each day in 2009.

- Five billion mobile phones were in use around the world in 2010.

- A fully analyzed human genome is about 1 terabyte of data.

- A wireless sensor that assesses a single cow's health transmits 200 megabytes of data per year.

- In 2008 the number of Internet-connected devices passed the number of people on the earth.

- Cisco Systems estimated that at the end of 2011, twenty typical households generated more Internet traffic than all Internet users did in 2008.

- McKinsey & Company estimates that, in almost every sector of the US economy, companies with more than one thousand employees store, on average, more information than the Library of Congress does.

Big data and analytics based on it promise to change virtually every industry and business function over the next decade. Any organization—and any individual within it—that gets started early with big data can gain a significant competitive edge. Just as early analytical competitors in the small data era moved out ahead of their competitors and built a sizable competitive edge, the time is now for firms and organizations to seize the big-data opportunity.

The potential of big data is enabled by ubiquitous computing and data-gathering devices; sensors and microprocessors will soon be everywhere. Virtually every mechanical or electronic device can leave a trail that describes its performance, location, or state. These devices, and the people who use them, communicate through the Internet—which leads to another vast data source. When all these bits are combined with those from other media—wireless and wired telephony, cable, satellite, and so forth—the future of data appears even bigger.

The availability of all this data means that virtually every business or organizational activity can be viewed as a big data problem or initiative. Manufacturing, in which most machines already have one or more microprocessors, is increasingly a big-data environment. Consumer marketing, with myriad customer touchpoints and click-streams, is already a big data problem. Google has even described its self-driving car as a big-data project.

CEOs like Gary Loveman at Caesars Entertainment (he's known for saying, "Do we think, or do we know?"), Jeff Bezos at Amazon ("We never throw away data"), and Reid Hoffman at LinkedIn ("Web 3.0 is about data") are publicly on record that analytical thinking and decision making is a route to organizational success and personal fortune.

All organizations in all industries will need to make sense of the onslaught of data. They'll need people who can do the detailed analysis of it—these people go by different names, but are *quants*, and this book is not meant for them. And they'll need people who can make good decisions and take actions based on the results—this is who we are writing to, the non-analysts, nonquantitative people in organizations who have to work with and make decisions based on quantitative data and analysis.

What We Hope You Get from This Book

As authors, we bring somewhat different backgrounds to this subject, but we share the goal of expanding the use of analytical thinking in business and society, and especially with helping *non-quants* become better consumers of data. Tom is not a serious quant himself—as a sociologist by academic background, his statistical skills are relatively modest—but he's an authority on analytics and their use in business. He has been researching, writing, teaching, and consulting with organizations about how to build analytical capabilities for a couple of decades. His experience working with managers and helping them use analytics is the foundation for writing this book. Additionally, he is the lead author on the best-selling books *Competing on Analytics* and *Analytics at Work*, which are focused on how big companies use analytics in their business strategies. With *Keeping Up with the Quants*, he shifts his focus to how individuals can build their analytical skills and orientations.

Jinho, with his academic background in business and statistics, came naturally to his role as an earnest quant. He has been researching how to use analytical methods to address various issues in business and society. Also, he has developed and run an education program for building individuals' analytical skills. Jinho is a professor of business and statistics in Korea and the author of six books, including *100 Common Senses in Statistics* and *Freak Statistics*, that are designed to help the nonstatistician understand and be more "literate" with statistical information.

This book will make you a better consumer of data, and will make you more conversant in analytics. It will make it easier for you to work with the quants and have meaningful discussions with them about the analyses they perform. It will enable you to speak the language of quantitative analysis and ask the right kinds of questions. It may even inspire you to become a quant!

An Informed Consumer of Analytics

There are many ways that managers, working closely with the quantitative analysts in their organizations, can use analytics to enhance their decisions. Let's take a recent decision that Jennifer Joy made at

Cigna—a leading health service company. Joy is vice president of Clinical Operations, and she runs a large call center for the company. The call center works with Cigna's customers to improve their health and wellness, particularly if they have a chronic condition, such as diabetes or heart disease, that requires ongoing treatment. Jen is a nurse by background, not an analyst. But she has an MBA and is a believer in the importance of analytical thinking. Her example shows how defining a problem and knowing the right questions to ask—two key aspects of thinking analytically—helped her save money for the company and her customers.

A key decision in Joy's operation is how much time to spend with Cigna customers on chronic-condition management—coaching them on how to avoid acquiring a disease or how to limit its progression. She wants to be sure that she is both providing value to customers, and controlling costs for Cigna. A key outcome variable for her is whether or not Cigna's customers are admitted or readmitted to the hospital. At one point, she had dozens of pages of monthly reports that showed the frequency of hospital readmissions. The percentages went up and down, but Joy was never sure what was driving them. "I got pages and pages of metrics," Joy said, "but they were just data—they didn't answer the 'So what?' question." The real question she wanted to answer was whether the calls with Cigna customers were really making a difference to their health and hospitalizations.

To get a better idea of cause-and-effect relationships between chronic-condition management activities and hospitalization rates, Joy sought out help from some analytics experts at Cigna. Michael Cousins heads the analytics group, and he and some colleagues began working with Joy to delve more deeply into the problem. Michael noted, "Jen may not understand all the details behind the cause-effect methodology, but she is logical, inquisitive, and asks smart questions. She may not be highly quantitative, but she's very analytically oriented." She's just the kind of decision maker that an analytics group loves to work with.

Cousins's group at Cigna specializes in aligning the analytical methodology with the business need. Cousins and his colleagues agreed with Joy that the pages of hospitalization rates weren't very useful, since they didn't answer her cause-and-effect business question about the impact her clinicians were having on health and hospitalizations. In other words, the prior reports showing upticks and downticks didn't use a methodology that was linked to her business question; there wasn't a credible comparison or reference group to use as the basis for decision making. For example, the prior reports didn't adjust for the risk levels of patients' situations—some sick people are sicker than others. Cousins's group developed a *matched case control* methodology, matching each patient with another who had similar health status, demographics, lifestyle, and geography. One customer of each matched pair received chronic-condition management coaching, and the other didn't, so Joy could determine just how effective the coaching was. Cousins pointed out, "It took some courage on her part to investigate whether these interventions—the main purpose of Jen's organization—were really working, but she didn't hesitate to find out the truth."

The results suggested that certain call center interventions weren't as helpful as anticipated for many types of diseases, but were more effective for others that they didn't anticipate. For the former group, Joy took action and decided to shorten the length of the calls for customers with certain diseases until it could be determined whether they were helpful at all. For the latter group, her team is expanding and redeploying call center staff to more value-adding activity with customers. She's working with Cousins's group on other analytics projects, including controlled experiments that test different coaching approaches, such as engaging more deeply with a customer's doctor. Rather than relying on gut instinct to know what works, she's embraced—in a dramatic fashion—the idea of structured analytics, such as *test and learn* pilot programs doing twenty or thirty tests per year.

Jennifer Joy was always analytically minded, but through the partnership with the analytics staff, she now has analytical tools at her disposal to execute on what's been in her mind so she can make fact-based decisions. And while the ideal way to treat disease over the telephone remains undiscovered, at least Cigna is spending less money on approaches that don't work and more money where there's proof that they do work. For his part, Michael Cousins and his group have also benefited from working with Joy and other analytically minded executives at Cigna. They've become much better at expressing the results of analyses in business terms and communicating what they mean for customers and financial outcomes.

So this book is for the Jennifer Joys of the world, not the Michael Cousinses. We are not proposing that you become a full-fledged quantitative analyst or data scientist. That would require a lot more study than reading this book, and not everybody has the interest or ability to pursue such roles. Instead, we want you to be data- and analytics savvy—to demand them, to use them in your job, to make decisions on the basis of them, and to be an advocate for them within your organization. We want people to say about you, "He's passionate about data," or, like Jen Joy at Cigna, "She's not a data geek herself, but she understands and appreciates the work they do." We don't want you to do complex data analyses yourself, but we would like you to be an intelligent consumer of them—helping to frame the decision, asking questions about the data and the methodology, working to understand the results, and using them to improve outcomes for your organization. To paraphrase Xiao-Li Meng, head of the Statistics Department at Harvard, we're not trying in this book to get you to become an expert winemaker (the term he uses for statistics PhDs), but rather a connoisseur of fine wine.[1]

At most times in the past, it was much more difficult to be an effective consumer of analytics without understanding a great deal about how they were created. But this situation has changed dramatically. Now, just as you don't have to know much about how an internal combustion engine works to be a good driver, you often don't need to know how the statistics were computed to use them in making decisions. Analytical software does more and more of the heavy lifting, sometimes even deciding what statistical analyses should be performed given the attributes of your data and variables. Some new analytics software (specifically from the company SAS) has a "What Does It Mean?" feature that explains in straightforward text what a correlation means or what method was used to compute a statistical forecast.

Despite the need for great consumers of analytics, thus far there has been no book specifically written, in nontechnical and simple terms, to develop the analytical skill levels of novices. This book describes what analytics are, shows how to implement analytics with many real-world cases, and suggests ways to improve your analytical capabilities. It should make you substantially better at understanding analytics yourself and should transform you into someone who can communicate effectively with others about analytical solutions to problems in organizations. According to the McKinsey Global Institute's report on big data in 2011, we'll need over 1.5 million more data-savvy managers to take advantage of all the data our society generates.[2] We hope you will become one of them.

The Importance of Analytics in Decision Making

Decisions in businesses and organizations can be based on a wide variety of factors, including personal experience, intuition, testing, or analytics and data. As in the book *Moneyball,* about the application of analytics to professional baseball, employing analytical decision making doesn't guarantee a positive outcome; the Oakland A's didn't win every game in the season described in the book or any subsequent season. However, analytics can provide a small edge to those who employ them. Oakland continues to do better than one might expect, given its miserly payroll. Of course, it is also possible for a decision maker to make a good decision using only experience and intuition—particularly in circumstances where he or she has a great deal of experience with the issue at hand. However, in almost every walk of life, there is evidence that analytical decision making is more accurate and precise and produces better decision outcomes.[3] In professional baseball, almost every team now employs the analytical approaches pioneered by the Oakland A's. Even the New York Yankees—who once took pride in their non-analytical approach to selecting players and game strategies—now employ twenty-one baseball statisticians.

In business, traditional analytics are primarily used to support internal decisions within organizations—questions like, "What should we charge for this product?" or "What promotion is likely to make this customer buy something from us?" Analytics in big data environments are often used to generate new products or features for customers—such as the PageRank algorithm for search at Google, the "People You May Know" feature in the social networking site LinkedIn, or the development of new games at Zynga. These are still a form of decision—either by the company itself or by a company's customer; for example, "Which people should I network with?" on LinkedIn. (The list "What Types of Business Decisions Can Be Made Analytically?" provides more examples.) And that's only scratching the surface. One could create similar lists for other industries and sectors—government, health care, sports, to name a few.

When a decision maker evaluates the alternatives, he or she takes into account the information from two sources: one from quantitative

What Types of Business Decisions Can Be Made Analytically?

Marketing

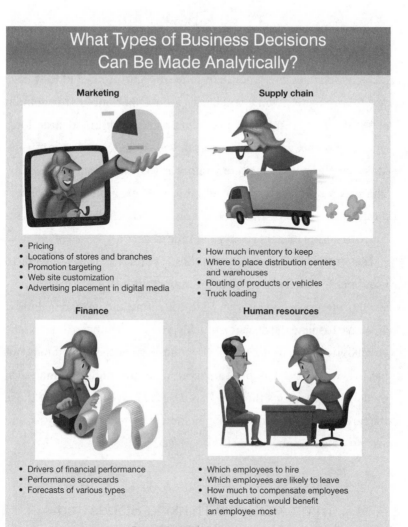

- Pricing
- Locations of stores and branches
- Promotion targeting
- Web site customization
- Advertising placement in digital media

Supply chain

- How much inventory to keep
- Where to place distribution centers and warehouses
- Routing of products or vehicles
- Truck loading

Finance

- Drivers of financial performance
- Performance scorecards
- Forecasts of various types

Human resources

- Which employees to hire
- Which employees are likely to leave
- How much to compensate employees
- What education would benefit an employee most

Research and development

- Which product features are most desired by customers
- How effective a particular product is
- Which product design is most appealing

analyses and the other from nonquantitative sources. Nonquantitative sources are those from intuition, experience, rules of thumb, hearsay, and guessing. These can sometimes be useful, but they have several problems. Even if you have a lot of experience in the domain of the decision, it might not be representative of broad situations. Guessing is always risky. In general, you should mistrust intuition. Most people value it much too highly as a guide to decision making. There is a whole school of economics, for example—called *behavioral economics*—based on the recognition that people are not good intuitive decision makers about economic issues.

Despite the advantages of analytics, it's still not always sensible to use them for a decision. If it's not important or it's a matter of personal preference, don't bother with collecting and analyzing data. If you have to make the decision quickly, you may not have time to take an analytical approach. And if it's a one-time decision, you may not feel it's worth the trouble to gather data and build an analytical model. The decisions that work well with analytics, then, are those that are made repeatedly, allow for some time to do the analysis, and are important enough to justify an investment.

Three Analytical Thinking Stages and How to Apply Them

The core of this book describes three major stages of analytical thinking. A chapter is devoted to each one, along with examples of analytical work in which a particular stage is particularly important. Figure 1-1 shows the three stages and the steps within them.

Chapter 2 covers the first stage, *framing the problem*. Framing the problem involves defining the question the analytics will answer and the decision to be made on the basis of the result. You can imagine

FIGURE 1-1

The three stages and six steps of quantitative analysis

Framing the problem

1. Problem recognition   2. Review of previous findings

Solving the problem

3. Modeling   4. Data collection   5. Data analysis

Communicating and acting on results

6. Results presentation and action

that it's a pretty important step; if you frame the problem incorrectly, no amount of data or sophisticated analysis will get you to the right place. There are two steps within framing the problem—one is *problem recognition*, and the other is *review of previous findings*. You'll see in chapter 2 that once you think you have recognized and defined the problem to be solved with analytics, you can probably find some aspect of the problem that has already been addressed by someone—and that usually helps you frame it better.

The second stage, the focus of chapter 3, is probably what you are thinking is the primary one—*solving the problem*. It's the stage in which you decide what variables are going to be in your model, collect data that measure those variables, and then actually do the data analysis. Assuming you're not a quant yourself and don't aspire to become one, you may work with quantitative analysts to do a lot of these activities. However, it's still very useful to know what the key activities are and generally how they are conducted. You may not solve the problem yourself, but your questions and insights will go a long way toward providing a better and more useful solution.

Chapter 4 looks at the third and final stage, which is just as important as the other two but is often neglected—*results presentation and action*. How you communicate about analytics is critical to whether anything is actually done with them. If a decision maker (perhaps you) doesn't understand what analyses have been done and what the results mean, he or she won't be comfortable making a decision based on them. So you might as well not have gone through the first couple of steps. And in this attention-challenged world that we live in today, communicating analytical results in an interesting, attention-getting way is particularly important. You can no longer present your results in a report full of black-and-white numbers and expect that anyone will do anything with them.

The chapters that follow look at some more specific issues related to thinking analytically. Chapter 5 discusses how you can use creativity in analytical work—they are not incompatible at all! Chapter 6 addresses some different ways that you can build your own analytical capabilities, should you be inclined to do so. And chapter 7 describes some effective ways that non-quant consumers of analytics can work effectively with quants to arrive at better decisions. Needless to say, it's a two-way street. Throughout are a number of examples, from all walks of life, showing how analytics can be used to solve problems (or not—see "The Danger of *Not* Thinking Analytically"). You'll also find worksheets with detail on how to apply analytics, as well as sections that highlight simple ways you can apply analytical thinking right away.

The Danger of *Not* Thinking Analytically

We learn from both negative and positive examples, but the negative ones are always more dramatic, so let's describe one of those. And nothing could be more dramatic than the case of Joe Cassano, who almost singlehandedly brought down a massive company and with it the United States—heck, the world—economy.

What did Cassano do, and what did he not know about analytics? You may remember something about him when we mention his position: head of AIG Financial Products (AIGFP), a small, four-hundred-person unit of the (formerly) giant insurance company AIG. What he did was to preside over the loss of a simply colossal amount of money—the exact amount is still in dispute, but it's somewhere around $85 billion dollars—which was the amount that US taxpayers had to pony up to keep AIG alive and to let it pay its debts. Cassano wasn't the only person to lose the money, but as the muckraking reporter Matt Taibbi wrote in *Rolling Stone*, he was "Patient Zero of the global economic meltdown."[a] Taibbi also described him as "a pudgy, balding Brooklyn College grad with beady eyes and way too much forehead," but that is not part of our story. If he'd made lots of money instead of losing it, we're sure his appearance would have improved.

Where do analytics and quantitative reasoning—or, more accurately, the lack of it—come in? AIGFP lost all of that money through selling a financial product called *credit default swaps* (CDSs), or insurance policies on the value of mortgage-backed derivatives. Gretchen Morgenson, a *New York Times* reporter, noted shortly after these events, "Although America's housing collapse is often cited as having caused the crisis, the system was vulnerable because of intricate financial contracts known as credit derivatives, which insure debt holders against default. They are fashioned privately and beyond the ken of regulators—sometimes even beyond the understanding of executives peddling them."[b]

Cassano was apparently one of those executives who didn't understand. Both the derivatives and the CDSs were complex products based on math and statistics—faulty math and statistics, as it turned out. If the recipients of the mortgages stopped being able to pay back the loans, the derivatives would become worthless and AIG would be stuck with paying their holders the insured value of the derivative. Needless to say at this point, that's exactly what happened.

Michael Lewis describes the core of the problem in AIGFP's business unit in *Vanity Fair*:

How and why their miracle became a catastrophe, A.I.G. F.P.'s traders say, is a complicated story, but it begins simply: with a change in the way decisions were made, brought about by a change in its leadership. At the end of 2001 its second C.E.O., Tom Savage, retired, and his former deputy, Joe Cassano, was elevated. Savage is a trained mathematician who understood the models used by A.I.G. traders to price the risk they were running—and thus ensure that they were fairly paid for it. He enjoyed debates about both the models and the merits of A.I.G. F.P.'s various trades. Cassano knew a lot less math and had much less interest in debate.[c]

Cassano didn't worry about whether the underlying risk and pricing models were accurate or not. He didn't ask the tough questions of the AIG and Wall Street analysts who had developed the models. He simply sold lots and lots of CDSs to anyone who would buy them. The possibility that they were based on false assumptions—notably that the people taking out these low-quality mortgage loans would actually be able to pay them back—never seemed to occur to him. Or if it did, he didn't seem to worry about it.

a. Matt Taibbi, "AIG and the Long Con," *Rolling Stone*, March 23, 2009.

b. Gretchen Morgenson, "Behind Insurer's Crisis, Blind Eye to a Web of Risk," *New York Times*, September 27, 2008.

c. Michael Lewis, "The Man Who Crashed the World," *Vanity Fair*, August 2009, http://www.vanityfair.com/politics/features/2009/08/aig200908.

For novices, studying by themselves to enhance analytical capability is not easy. We've set up a website (http://keeping upwiththequants.weebly.com) where readers can ask any question about analytical knowledge, techniques, or the problems they are facing in solving specific problems. Please feel free to post any question there. Also on the website are detailed analyses of some of cases described in the text. We occasionally refer to this website in the text.

2

Framing the Problem

While there are many different types of quantitative analysis, they all have certain key features and steps in common. As we noted in chapter 1, a quantitative analysis follows the following three stages and six steps:

FRAMING THE PROBLEM

- Problem recognition

- Review of previous findings

SOLVING THE PROBLEM

- Modeling and variable selection

- Data collection

- Data analysis

COMMUNICATING AND ACTING ON RESULTS

- Results presentation and action

In this chapter and chapters 3 and 4, we'll describe each stage and step individually, and provide a couple of examples of quantitative analyses that cover all six steps, but feature the particular stage of analysis being discussed in the chapter. At the end of each of the three chapters we'll lay out two examples—generally one from business and one involving society in general or personal experience—that illustrate how all six steps were employed in an analysis, but again focus in particular on one stage of the analysis. Our three-stage, six-step process isn't the only way to do analytics (for example, there is a Six Sigma methodology for analyzing variation in product quality yielding no more than 3.4 defects per million products produced), but we expect that most analytical experts would agree with it, and it's broad enough to encompass a lot of different types of business problems and analyses.

The Problem Recognition Step

A quantitative analysis starts with recognizing a problem or decision and beginning to solve it. In decision analysis, this step is called *framing*, and it's one of the most critical parts of a good decision process. There are various sources that lead to this first step, including:

1. Problem recognition

- Pure curiosity (common sense, observation of events)

- Experiences on the job

- Need for a decision or action

- Current issues requiring attention (of a person, an organization, or a nation)

- Building on, or contesting, existing theories or past research

- Accepting of project offers or determining availability funding

Note that at this step, the analytics are yet to come. The decision to forge ahead with some sort of analysis may be driven by a hunch or an intuition. The standard of evidence at this point is low. Of course, the whole point of a quantitative analysis is to eventually apply some data and test your hunch. That's the difference between analytical thinkers and others: they test their hunches with data and analysis.

The most important thing in the problem recognition stage is to fully understand what the problem is and why it matters. The answers to these two questions not only make it clear what can be accomplished by solving the problem, but also facilitate the ensuing stages.

Identifying the Stakeholders for the Analysis

Perhaps obviously, the individuals involved at this step are primarily managers and decision makers—the "owners" of the business or organizational problem. However, even at this stage their efforts can be greatly aided by the presence of experienced quantitative analysts who understand the business problem, the decision process, and the likely quantitative approaches to be employed. If all of that knowledge can't be found within one person, you may need a team that jointly possesses it.

It's worth some serious thinking at this step about who the stakeholders are for the analysis you plan to undertake, and how they're

Stakeholder Analysis Worksheet

If you can't answer most of these questions with a "yes," your project may be in trouble from the beginning:

1. Is it clear what executives have a stake in the success of your quantitative analysis project?

2. Have they been briefed on the problem and the outlines of the solution?

3. Do they have the ability to provide the necessary resources and to bring about the business changes needed to make the project successful?

4. Do they generally support the use of analytics and data for decision making?

5. Does the proposed analytical story and method of communicating it coincide with their typical way of thinking and deciding?

6. Do you have a plan for providing regular feedback and interim results to them?

---

feeling about the problem (see the "Stakeholder Analysis Worksheet"). Do you have stakeholders who can take action on the results? Are they feeling skeptical that the problem even exists? Are they likely to be persuaded to do something even if the analysis is bulletproof?

The tendency of analysts is often to jump right into the analysis without thinking of stakeholders. The more confident they are in their analytical skills, the less they may worry about who will ultimately be the audience for the results and the "deciders" about whether to take action.

If you're persuaded of the need for stakeholder management for your analytical project, some of the common steps involved in that process include:

1. Identifying all stakeholders

2. Documenting stakeholders needs

3. Assessing and analyzing stakeholders interest/influence

4. Managing stakeholders expectations

5. Taking actions

6. Reviewing status and repeating[1]

A stakeholder analysis can identify who are the primary decision makers, and how they are most likely to be persuaded by the results from the analysis. Even the most rigorous and bulletproof analysis approach will be of little use if it does not persuade a decision maker to act. In fact, it may even make sense to use a questionable approach from a methodological standpoint if that is the only evidence a decision maker will trust.

For example, Rob Duboff runs a marketing research and strategy firm called HawkPartners. In general, he believes in the value of quantitative research whenever possible. However, he has learned that some executives don't understand quantitative approaches to learning customer wants and needs, and believe much more in qualitative approaches such as focus groups—convening a small group of customers or potential customers, asking them what they think about a company's products and services, and observing and recording their responses. Now Duboff knows that focus groups are methodologically suspect. It's pretty well known in the marketing research field that customers are likely to tell you what you want to hear, and the fact that they say they like something doesn't mean they would actually buy it. These problems can be mitigated by a skillful discussion leader, but focus group results are not projectable to a wider universe. However, Duboff feels that any research is better than none, and if evidence from a focus group would be trusted and acted on by an executive—and more quantitative results would not—he conducts the focus group.

In a similar sense, the stakeholders for the decision can help to determine the form of output and results presentation. Humans differ in their preferences for seeing quantitative results; some prefer rows and columns of numbers, some prefer graphics, and some prefer text describing the numbers. It's important to elicit those preferences at a relatively early stage. If the results are going to be used not by humans but by a computer—and this is increasingly the case as more and more decisions are automated or partially automated—then it makes little sense to deliberate over the ideal visual format. Just feed it the numbers it thrives on!

It may also be the case that certain analytical approaches can help to involve stakeholders throughout the analysis. For example, at Cisco Systems, a forecasting project addressed the possibility that substantially more accurate forecasts were possible through statistical methods (we'll describe the six steps for this example at the end of chapter 7). Some Cisco managers were supportive of the project, but others doubted that better forecasts were possible. Anne Robinson, who managed the project, employed an "agile" methodology for the project, creating new deliverables every few weeks and presenting them to project stakeholders. The more incremental approach to solving the problem helped stakeholders buy into the new approach. Eventually it became clear to even the skeptical managers that the new forecasting approach was far more accurate and could be done more quickly and for more products than the previous nonanalytical approach.

Focusing on Decisions

We have found it helpful in the problem-recognition stage to focus on specific decisions that will be made as a result of the analysis. There are many reasons for this focus. One key reason is that a decision focus makes all participants realize that that is the reason for the quantitative analysis; it's not an idle exercise. Another is that focusing on the decision to be made will help to identify a key stakeholder: the person or group that will make a decision based on the analysis. A third key reason is that if there are no decisions envisioned, it may not be worth doing the analysis.

For example, Mike Thompson, the head of First Analytics, an analytics services firm, describes a meeting he had with a client at the problem-recognition stage. The client, a restaurant chain, believed that the primary focus of the analysis was product profitability. Client executives wanted First Analytics to determine how profitable each menu item was. Mike also subscribes to the idea of focusing on decisions, so he asked the client managers what decisions they would make as a result of the profitability analyses. There was a long silence. One executive suggested that the primary decision would be whether to keep items on the menu or not. Another pointed out, however, that the chain had not eliminated a single menu item over the past twenty years. After some further discussion, the client team decided that perhaps the focus of analysis should be menu item pricing, rather than profitability. "We have changed prices since our founding," one executive observed.

What Type of Analytical Story Are You Telling?

Once you've decided what decisions you are going to make, you can begin to think about how you are going to provide answers or insights for that decision. We'll talk in chapter 4 about *telling a story with data*, which is the best way to communicate results to nonanalytical people. At this point, you need to begin thinking about what kind of story it is and how you will tell it, although many of the details of the story will come later in the analysis process. Stories are, of course, how numbers talk to people. There are at least six types of quantitative analytical stories; each of them is described below, along with an example or two.

THE CSI STORY. Some quantitative analyses are like police procedural television programs; they attempt to solve a business problem with quantitative analysis. Some operational problem crops up, and data are used to confirm the nature of the issue and find the solution. This situation often does not require deep statistical analysis, just good data and reporting approaches. It is often encountered in online businesses, where customer clickstreams provide plenty of data—often too much—for analysis.

One expert practitioner of the CSI story approach is Joe Megibow, vice president and general manager of online travel company Expedia's US business. Joe was previously a Web analytics maven—and he still is—but his data-based problem-solving approaches have led to a variety of impressive promotions.

Many of the Expedia investigations involve understanding the reasons behind lost online sales. One particular CSI story involved lost revenue on hotel payment transactions. Analysis of data suggested that after a customer had selected a hotel, filled in the travel and billing information, then clicked the "Buy Now" button, a percentage of the sales transactions were not being completed successfully. Megibow's team investigated the reason for the failures, again using Web metrics data and server log files throughout the process.

Apparently, the "Company" field under the customer's name was causing a problem. Some customers interpreted it as the name of the bank that supplied their credit card, and then they also supplied the bank's address in the billing address fields. This caused the transaction to fail with the credit card processor. Simply removing the "Company" field immediately raised profits for Expedia by $12 million. Megibow says that Expedia has explored many of these CSI-like stories, and they almost always yield substantial financial or operational benefits.

Sometimes the CSI stories do involve deeper quantitative and statistical analysis. One member of Megibow's team was investigating which customer touchpoints were driving online sales transactions. The analyst used the *Cox regression model*—an approach originally used to determine which patients would die and which would live over certain time periods—of "survival analysis." The analysis discovered that the simpler prior models were not at all correct about what marketing approaches were really leading to a sale. Megibow commented, "We didn't know we were leaving money on the table."[2]

THE EUREKA STORY. The Eureka story is similar to the CSI story, except that it typically involves a purposeful approach to a particular problem (as opposed to stumbling over the problem) to examine a major change in an organization's strategy or business model. It tends to be a longer story with a greater degree of analysis over time. Sometimes Eureka stories also involve other analytical story types, just because the results are so important to the organizations pursuing them.

At Expedia again, for example, one Eureka story involved eliminating change/cancel fees from online hotel, cruise, and car rental reservations. Until 2009, Expedia and its competitors all charged up to $30 for a change or cancellation—above and beyond the penalties the hotel imposed. Expedia and other online bookers' rates were typically much lower than booking directly with a hotel, and customers were willing to tolerate change/cancel fees.

However, by 2009 it had become apparent that the fees had become a liability. Expedia's rates were closer to those of the hotels' own rates, so the primary appeal of Expedia had become convenience—and change/cancel fees were not convenient. Analysts looked at customer satisfaction rates, and they were particularly low for customers who had to pay the fees. Expedia's call center representatives were authorized to waive the change/cancel fees for only one reason: a death in the customer's family. A look at the number of waivers showed double-digit growth for the past three years. Either there was a death epidemic, or customers had figured out they could get their money back this way.

Expedia executives realized the market had changed, but change/cancel fees represented a substantial source of revenue. They wondered if the fees were eliminated, would conversion (completed sale) rates go up? In April of 2009, they announced a temporary waiver of fees for the month (a bit of a mad scientist testing story, described below). Conversion rates immediately rose substantially. Executives felt that they had enough evidence to discontinue the fees, and the rest of the industry followed suit.

Across town in Seattle lies Zillow, a company that distributes information about residential real estate. Zillow is perhaps best known to quant jocks for its "Zestimates," a proprietary algorithm that generates estimates of home values. But, like Expedia, Zillow's entire culture is based on data and analysis—not surprisingly, since the company was founded by Rich Barton, who also founded Expedia.

One of Zillow's Eureka stories involved a big decision to change how it made its money from relationships with real estate agents. Zillow began to work with agents in 2008, having previously been focused on consumers. One aspect of its agent-related business model was selling advertising by agents and delivering leads to them. Zillow charged the agents for the leads, but the value per lead was not enough in the view of executives. Chloe Harford, a Zillow executive who heads product management and strategy, was particularly focused on figuring out the right model for increasing lead value and optimizing the pricing of leads.

Harford, who has a PhD in volcanology, or the study of volcanoes, is capable of some pretty sophisticated mathematical analysis. However, she and her colleagues initially relied on what she calls "napkin math" to explore other ways to generate more leads and price them fairly to agents. In April 2010, Zillow created a new feature—immediately copied by competitors—involving selling advertising to agents. It created many more customer contacts than before, and allowed the consumer to contact the agent directly. Zillow also introduced a sophisticated algorithm for pricing leads to agents that attempts to calculate the economic value of the lead, with an estimate of conversion rates. Competitors also do this to some degree, but probably not to the level of sophistication that Zillow does. The leads and pricing of them are so important that Harford and her colleagues frequently test different approaches of them with some of the Mad Scientist testing approaches described below. In short, Zillow's Eureka stories are intimately tied into its business model and its business success.

THE MAD SCIENTIST STORY. We're all familiar with the use of scientific testing in science-based industries such as pharmaceuticals. Drug companies test their products on a group of test subjects, while giving a placebo to members of a control group. They pay careful attention to ensure that people are randomly assigned to either the test or control group, so there are no major differences between the groups that might impact the drug's effectiveness. It's a powerful analytical tool because it's usually as close as we can come to causation—the knowledge that what is being tested in the test group is driving the outcome in a causal fashion.

Rigorous testing is no longer just the province of white-coated scientists; it is now an analytical approach that every large organization can employ. There is broadly available software that leads managers or analysts through the testing process. Companies can now base important decisions on real, scientifically valid experiments. In the past, any foray into randomized testing (the random assignment to groups that we mentioned above) meant employing or engaging a PhD in statistics or a "design of experiments" expert. Now, a quantitatively trained MBA can oversee the process, assisted by software that will help determine what sizes of groups are necessary, which sites to use for testing and controls, and whether any changes resulting from experiments are statistically significant.

The mad scientist stories are particularly well suited to organizations like retailers (that have a lot of stores) and banks (that have a lot of branches). That makes it easy to try things out in some locations and use others as controls. It's also quite easy to do testing on websites, where you can send some customers to one version of a Web page, send other customers to a different version, and see if the results are significantly different (called *A/B testing* in the Web analytics field).

Some examples of mad scientist stories include:[3]

- Do lobster tanks sell more lobsters at Food Lion supermarkets? The answer is apparently yes if the store was one in which customers already bought lobsters (i.e., they were relatively upscale), and no if the store didn't attract lobster-buying customers to begin with.

- Does a Sears store inside a Kmart sell more than all-Kmart? Sears Holdings chairman Eddie Lampert is a big fan of randomized testing and has tested a variety of such combinations. We don't know the answer to this particular question, but we're guessing that if the answer were a definitive yes, we would have seen a lot more of these blended stores.

- Are the best sales results at the Red Lobster seafood restaurant chain achieved from a low-, medium-, or high-cost remodel of restaurants—and should the exterior or the interior be the primary focus? The result, according to Red Lobster executives, was that the medium-cost interior remodel paid off best. Exterior remodels brought a lot of new customers in, but if they saw that the interiors hadn't been redone as well, they didn't come back.

THE SURVEY STORY. Surveys are a classic method of quantitative research. The survey analyst observes phenomena that have already happened or are happening now. The analyst doesn't try to manipulate the outcome—only to observe, codify, and analyze it. Typically the surveyor seeks to understand what traits or variables observed in the survey are statistically related to other traits. The simplest example would be if we asked a sample of customers of a particular product various things about themselves, including demographic information like gender and age. If we also asked what products they liked, we could then determine whether men like certain products more than women, or whether certain products are more likely to be liked by younger people.

Surveys are popular and relatively easy to carry out. However, we have to remember that the results and stories based on them can vary considerably based on how questions are asked and how they vary (or not) over time. For example, the US Census has worked for literally decades on questions about the race of US citizens. The number of racial categories in census surveys keeps expanding; in the 2010 census there were fifteen choices, including "some other race." That was a popular choice for the more than 50 million Latino US citizens, 18 million of whom checked the "Other" box.[4] If there is that much confusion about race, imagine what difficulties survey researchers can have with slippery topics such as politics, religion, social attitudes, and sexual behavior.

We also have to remember that just because two variables in a survey analysis are related, they may not be causally related. We'll have more to say about this issue in chapter 6, but for now we'll just point out that there may well be other variables that you're not looking at that might be the causal factor driving the phenomena you care about.

Survey stories often involve asking people about their beliefs and attitudes, but they don't have to involve people. Take, for example, this survey of airplanes conducted during World War II, related in a classic statistics textbook:

> During the Second World War it was necessary to keep planes in action as much as possible, so it was decided to see if the number of time-consuming engine overhauls could be reduced without risk. A retrospective survey was made of planes that were lost, and contrary to all expectations, it was found that the number of planes lost as a result of engine troubles was greatest right after overhaul, and actually decreased as the time since overhaul grew longer. This result led to a considerable increase in the intervals between overhauls, and needless to say, to important revisions in the manner of overhauling to make sure that all those nuts and bolts were really tightened up properly.[5]

If you're planning to do or analyze a survey, make sure that you've thought very carefully about the meanings of your survey questions or variables. A variable is any measured characteristic, with two or more levels or values, of properties of people, situations, and behaviors. Gender, test scores, room temperature, love, happiness, and team cohesiveness are good examples of variables.

Also, it's important to ensure that your survey sample is representative of the population you want to study. How you perform the survey can affect the sample. For example, if you want to survey young people's attitudes or behaviors, don't hire a survey firm that only contacts the members of the sample through landline telephones. That's a very typical approach, but we all know that many young people don't have, and don't ever intend to have, a landline. So they would be underrepresented in a sample that employs only landlines.[6]

THE PREDICTION STORY. Prediction stories are all about anticipating what will happen in the future. While it's pretty difficult to get good data about the future, taking data about the past and understanding the factors that drive past events is pretty straightforward for quantitative analytics. Typically this is referred to as *predictive analytics* or *predictive modeling.*

There are a variety of prediction stories that an analyst can construct. Below is a sample of possibilities; note how specific they are:

- *Offer response:* Which customers will respond to an e-mail of a free shipping offer within two business days with a purchase of $50 or more?

- *Cross-sell/upsell:* Which checking account customers with account balances over $2,000 will purchase a one-year CD with an interest rate of 1.5 percent, responding within one month, given a mail solicitation?

- *Employee attrition:* Which employees of more than six months who haven't yet signed up for the 401(k) program will resign from their jobs within the next three months?

There are many other predictive analytics possibilities. In business, a common approach to prediction is to determine what offer the customer is most likely to accept. The most sophisticated versions of this "next best offer" analytics are increasingly automated; no human needs to see the offer before it is made available to the customer, and there can be hundreds or thousands of different offers.

Microsoft, for example, has an incredible ability to dynamically tailor "offers" for its Bing search engine (the product is free, so Microsoft is just trying to get you to use it). The offers tempt you to try out Bing, to create a Bing search bar on your browser, to try a particular Bing feature, and so forth. The customization of the offer is based on a variety of factors—including your location, age, gender, and recent online activity—that it can determine from your cookies and other sources. If you have signed up for Microsoft Passport, the company has even more information about you that allows for targeting the offers even more effectively. Microsoft is able (facilitated by the Infor Epiphany Interaction Advisor software they use) to instantly compose a targeted e-mail the moment you click on an offer in your inbox; it all takes about 200 milliseconds. Microsoft says it works extremely well to lift conversion rates.

Often, prediction stories can be a bit of a fishing expedition. We don't know exactly what factors will allow us to predict something, so we try a lot of them and see what works. Sometimes the results are unexpected. For example, in the Microsoft Bing offers we've just described, the number of Microsoft Messenger buddies you have turns out to be a good predictor of whether you'll try out Bing.

At Google, the company wanted to predict what employee traits predicted high performance. Some analysis determined that the factors Google was originally using—grades in college and interview ratings—were poor predictors of performance. Since they weren't sure what factors would be important, they asked employees to answer a three-hundred-question survey. As Laszlo Bock, the head of People Operations at Google, noted: "We wanted to cast a very wide net. It is not unusual to walk the halls here and bump into dogs. Maybe people who own dogs have some personality trait that is useful."[7]

Bringing pets to work didn't prove to predict much of anything, but Google did find some unexpected predictors. For example, whether a job applicant had set a world or national record or had started a nonprofit organization or club were both associated with high performance. Google now asks questions about experiences like these on its online job interviews.

Of course, if the factors that predict something make no sense at all, it's a good idea to go back and recheck your data and your analysis. But actually looking at some data can outperform a human futurist's predictions much of the time. As a caution, remember that predictive stories use data from the past to tell stories about the future. If something in the world has changed since you did your analysis, the predictions may no longer hold.

THE "HERE'S WHAT HAPPENED" STORY. Stories that simply tell what happened using data are perhaps the most common of all. They provide the facts—how many products were sold when and where, what were the financials that were achieved last quarter, how many people did we hire last year. Since they are reporting-oriented stories that often don't use sophisticated math, it might seem that they would be easy to tell. However, the great rise in data within today's organizations has been mirrored by a similar rise in reports based on data. Therefore, it's sometimes difficult to get the attention of the intended audience for the reports you create or distribute.

This type of story is particularly well suited to visual displays of information. Suffice it to say that if you are providing reports in rows and columns of numbers, you aren't likely to get the attention you need. Many of us even tire today of colorful graphs and charts, but most people would say they are more worthy of attention than numbers on a page. Since chapter 4 is about communicating results, we'll say more about how to make this kind of report more interesting and attention-getting there.

The Scope of the Problem

By definition, a data-driven story and the quantitative analysis behind it can be somewhat narrow in scope, simply because it requires gathering data and applying it to a testable hypothesis (see "Examples of Testable Hypotheses"). It's difficult to gather data on very broad problems. However, it's important at this step not to prematurely limit the scope of the problem or decision. Thinking about the issue should be expansive, and you should have a number of alternative directions in mind. For example, if an organization recognizes a performance problem within a particular business unit or region, it should be open to a variety of causes of the problem—from customer dissatisfaction to operational issues to problems with products or services.

In the example of Transitions Optical at the end of this chapter, the problem recognition and framing step was prompted by a vague sense that marketing spending was too high, but the decision frame was expanded into one involving an overall optimization of marketing spending levels and media used.

We've referred to this first step in quantitative analysis as problem recognition, but it can also be an identification of opportunities. Joseph Jagger (1830–1892), a British engineer, realized that there was an opportunity to "break the bank" at the Monte Carlo casino.[8] Jagger gained his practical experience of mechanics working in Yorkshire's cotton manufacturing industry. He extended his experience to the behavior of a roulette wheel, speculating that its outcomes

Examples of Testable Hypotheses

- The type of products that a customer has bought from us in the past year is the best guide to what e-mailed offers he or she will respond positively to in the future.

- Years of education is a good predictor of the level of performance rating an employee will receive in knowledge work jobs.

- Price markdowns of 10 percent made in the week before a holiday are less effective than those made at other periods.

- An end-cap display is the most effective placement of our product in a retail store for lifting weekly sales.

- Our customers can be grouped into four distinct segments with regard to the products they buy.

- Our ability to raise prices on a class of consumer staple products without hurting demand is significantly lower during economic recessions.

- Our business units that have centralized inventory management facilities tend to maintain lower average days of inventory for their production processes.

were not purely random sequences but that mechanical imbalances might result in biases toward particular outcomes. What if there were imperfections in the roulette wheel that he could exploit to his advantage? He went to Monaco to test this concept.

There are thirty-seven numbers in a French/European roulette wheel: 1–36 and 0. When a wheel is spun once, the theoretical probability that each number will come out is equal to 1/37. Therefore the proportion of each resultant number in a large number of spins should be roughly 1/37. Jagger speculated that mechanical imbalances, if any, in wheels would cause specific numbers to appear more often than the probability of 1/37.

With these thoughts in mind, Jagger hired six clerks to observe the six roulette wheels at the legendary Beaux-Arts Casino in Monte Carlo, each covering a different wheel. Each had specific instructions to record all of the results that came from each spin. When he analyzed the results, Jagger found that five of the roulette wheels produced the random results that one would expect. On the sixth wheel, however, he found that nine particular numbers (7, 8, 9, 17, 18, 19, 22, 28, and 29) appeared more often than mere chance could account for. Jagger concluded that the wheel was biased—that is, imperfectly balanced. He accordingly placed his first bets on July 7, 1875, and quickly won a considerable amount of money (£14,000— equivalent to around sixty times that amount in 2012, or over $1.3 million, adjusted for inflation). The casino caught on to Jagger's betting strategy, and eventually neutralized it—but not before he had won the current equivalent of over $6 million. Quite an analytical opportunity!

Getting Specific About What You Want to Find Out

While it's important to think expansively early in the problem recognition step, by the end of it you'll need to have created a clear statement of the problem, with concrete definitions of the key items or variables you want to study. Here's why: it makes a big difference how things are defined in quantitative research. For example, let's say you were a television executive interested in learning what channels consumers watched. Two different analytical consultants have approached you with proposals to learn the answer. Just for fun you decide to hire both of them to see how their results compare.

One consultant proposes to ask consumers to record (using either an online or a paper form) the actual channels and programs watched each day for a week. The other suggests asking the survey respondents to rank the channels they generally watch on television over the last several months. Both have well-designed survey samples that represent the desired population.

While these two consultants are trying to solve very similar problems, they are likely to come back with very different results. The one who proposes that consumers record actual programs and channels watched each day is likely to get more accurate results, but the extra burden of recording is likely to mean a lower level of participation from the survey sample. (Nielsen Media Research, which does channel and program monitoring on an ongoing basis, has about a 50 percent dropout level, and its recording is automated.) The other problem with this consultant is that viewing patterns might be overly influenced by the particular season or programming offered during the particular week of the study.

The other study is likely to be less accurate, but since it covers a broader time period, it is less likely to be influenced by seasonal factors. Most importantly, the results of the two surveys will probably be so different as to be difficult to reconcile. That's why it's important to finish the problem recognition step with a clear idea about what you want to study.

Review of Previous Findings Step

Once the problem is recognized, all the previous findings connected to it should be investigated. This is still a step within the first stage of analysis (framing the problem) because investigating previous findings can help analysts and decision makers think about how the

2. Review of previous findings

problem has been structured thus far, and how it might be conceptualized in different ways. Quite often, analysts will discover something in the review of previous findings that will lead to a substantial revision of the problem recognition step. That in turn can lead to a different set of previous findings.

Basically at this step we are asking, "Has a story similar to this been told before?" If so, we can get ideas for our own analysis. The review of previous findings can suggest any of the following:

- What kind of story could we tell? Does it involve prediction, reporting, an experiment, a survey?

- What kind of data are we likely to want to look for?

- How have variables been defined before?

- What types of analyses are we likely to perform?

- How could we tell the story in an interesting way that is likely to get results, and different from past stories?

One of the key attributes of quantitative analysis (and of the scientific method more broadly) is that it draws on previous research and findings. For example, searching thorough the problem-related knowledge appearing in books, reports, and articles is very important in getting to the bottom of the problem. It may help to identify relevant variables and any association among the identified variables.

A complete review of any of the previous findings is a must in any given quantitative analysis. You cannot make something out of nothing in analytics. You may only begin to solve the problem once you have a total grasp of the previous findings. Just remember one thing: your problem is not as unique as you think, and it's likely that many people have already done just what you are trying to do. Do not reinvent the wheel; what you need to do is search, search, and search again. These days, by using a search engine like Google, you can easily muster up most of the material related to your issue. By just arranging and evaluating the material, you can identify a potential model or approach to solve the problem.

An example of a successful review of previous findings took place during World War II. Adolf Hitler had ordered the production of a powerful new rocket bomb called the V-2, and in 1944 the Luftwaffe began to terrify the citizens of London. Over the next few months, 1,358 V-2s, out of at least 3,172 rockets distributed over the various Allied targets, flew out of the sky and landed in London, resulting in the death of an estimated 7,250 military personnel and civilians.

During the attack on London, many observers asserted that the points of impact of the bombs were grouped in clusters. The British were interested in knowing whether the Germans could actually target their bomb hits or were merely limited to random hits. If the Germans could only randomly hit targets, then deployment throughout the countryside of various security installations would serve quite well to protect the nation. But if the Germans could actually target their bombs, then the British were faced with a more potent opponent; the deployment of security installations would do little to protect them. The British government engaged statistician R. D. Clarke to solve this question. Clarke applied a simple statistical test based on his review—or existing knowledge—of previous findings.

Clarke was aware that the *Poisson distribution* could be used to analyze the distribution of bombs. The Poisson distribution expresses the probability of a number of events occurring in a fixed period of time, area, or volume if these events occur with a known average rate. The only thing we have to know to specify the Poisson distribution is the mean number of occurrences. If the bombs are falling randomly, the number of bombs that hit any particular small area follows a Poisson distribution. For example, if the average number of bombs that hit is 1 bomb per area, we can easily calculate the probabilities that no bomb will hit, exactly 1 bomb will hit, exactly 2 bombs will hit, exactly 3 bombs will hit, and exactly 4 or more bombs will hit, just by plugging these numbers in the Poisson formula.

To measure the number of bombs that may hit any specifically defined small area, Clarke divided South London into 576 squares of one-quarter square kilometer each, and counted the numbers of squares containing 0, 1, 2, 3, etc., flying bombs. If the targeting was completely random, then the probability that a square is hit with 0, 1, 2, 3, etc., hits would be governed by a Poisson distribution. The actual fit of the Poisson pattern for the data was surprisingly good, which lent no support to the clustering hypothesis (see the website for this book). The British were relieved by Clarke's conclusion. Fortunately, the Germans surrendered in 1945 before the V-2 could do much more damage. (*Note:* Despite its inability to be guided effectively, that rocket became the technical basis of the US space program.)

Just as Clarke did when he realized that the problem of the falling bombs could be described by a Poisson distribution, you can go back and review the problem recognition step after you have reviewed previous findings (see "Some Methods for Reviewing Previous Findings"). You may find that you need to modify your story, your problem scope, your decision, or even your stakeholders. If you have revised those a bit, or if you're still happy with the original problem

Some Methods for Reviewing Previous Findings

- Do an Internet search for key terms related to your analysis.

- Consult a statistics textbook for analyses similar to the one you're proposing.

- Talk to analysts around your company to see if they've done something similar.

- Check your company's knowledge management system if it has one.

- Talk about the problem with analysts at other (but noncompetitive) companies.

- Attend a conference (or at least look online at conference agendas) on analytics to see if anyone else is presenting on related topics.

definition, you can consider your problem framed and move along to actually solving it using quantitative analysis.

Reframing the Problem

Although we've laid out the analytical problem-solving process as a linear one of six steps in three stages, it is nothing if not iterative. Every step sheds new light on the problem, and it's always a good idea to think about how the new knowledge might shed light on previous steps. Although you can't spend forever reexamining each step, it's worth some time thinking about what the review of previous findings suggests about framing the problem (the "Worksheet for Framing the Problem" can help).

Worksheet for Framing the Problem

Have you framed the problem well? If so, you should be able to answer all or most of these questions positively:

1. Have you defined a clear problem or opportunity to address what is important to your business or organization?

2. Have you considered multiple alternative ways to solve the problem?

3. Have you identified the stakeholders for the problem, and communicated with them extensively about it?

4. Are you confident that the way you plan to solve the problem will resonate with the stakeholders, and that they will use the results to make a decision?

5. Are you clear on what decision is to be made—and who will make it—on the basis of the results from your analysis once the problem is solved?

6. Have you started with a broad definition of the problem, but then narrowed it down to a very specific problem with clear phrasing on the question to be addressed, the data to be applied to it, and the possible outcomes?

7. Are you able to describe the type of analytical story that you want to tell in solving this particular problem?

8. Do you have someone who can help you in solving that particular type of analytical story?

9. Have you looked systematically to see whether there are previous findings or experience related to this problem either within or outside your organization?

10. Have you revised your problem definition based on what you have learned from your review of previous findings?

For a good example, Rama Ramakrishnan, a retail analytics expert who is now CEO of the start-up CQuotient, describes a situation suitable for reframing in one of his blog posts:[9]

> Take the "customer targeting" problem that arises in direct marketing. Customer targeting is about deciding which customers should be mailed (since mailing every customer is expensive). This is an old problem that has been studied by numerous researchers and practitioners. The most commonly used approach is as follows:
>
> 1. send a test mailing to a sample of customers
>
> 2. use the results of the test mailing to build a "response model" that predicts each customer's propensity to respond to the mailing as a function of their attributes, past history etc.
>
> 3. use this model to score each customer in the database and mail to the top scorers.
>
> This looks reasonable and may well be what the business cares about. But perhaps not.
>
> The words "response model" suggest that the mailing *caused* the customer to respond. In reality, the customer may have come into the store and made a purchase anyway (I am thinking of multichannel retailers and not pure-play catalog retailers.

For the latter, without the catalog, it may be impossible for customers to make a purchase so the word "response" may be appropriate).

What these response models really do is identify customers who are likely to shop rather than customers likely to shop as a result of the mailing. But maybe what management really wants is the latter. For those customers who are either going to shop anyway or not going to shop regardless of what is mailed to them, mailing is a waste of money and potentially costs customer goodwill too. What the business may really want is to identify those customers who will shop if mailed, but won't if not mailed.

This re-framing of the customer targeting problem and approaches for solving it are relatively recent. It goes by many names—uplift modeling, net lift modeling—and the academic work on it is quite minimal compared to traditional response modeling. Yet, for many retailers, this is a more relevant and useful way to frame and solve the customer targeting problem than doing it the old way.

In this example, a thorough review of previous findings might have revealed the recent work on uplift and net lift modeling, and that might occasion a reframing of the problem. Ramakrishnan suggests that in such situations with relatively new modeling approaches, "Since the new problem hasn't received enough attention (by definition), simple algorithms may yield benefits quickly."

We'll conclude this chapter on framing the problem with a couple of examples, one from business and one from law, in which the framing process was critical to the outcome. One is a good example of framing, and one is an example of incorrect framing. You haven't learned much yet about the steps beyond the framing stage, but we're confident that you can make sense of them in these examples.

Analytical Thinking Example: Transitions Optical

One of the most common analytical problems in business is deciding how much to spend on a specific activity. And that's a particularly difficult decision for marketing spending. The department store founder John Wanamaker—and some European retailers before him—are renowned for saying, "Half the money I spend on advertising is wasted; the trouble is I don't know which half." Today, however, companies can use quantitative analysis to find out which marketing expenditures are effective, and which are not—and what the most effective combination of marketing expenditures is. This is typically called *marketing mix analysis,* and it's increasingly popular for firms that sell to consumers.

PROBLEM RECOGNITION AND FRAMING. Transitions Optical, which offers photochromic lenses for glasses, was getting some pressure from its corporate parents (Transitions is jointly owned by PPG and Essilor) with regard to its level of marketing spending. PPG, in particular, isn't in the business of consumer marketing, so that parent was especially skeptical about the cost and value of advertising and promotion. There were specific questions about whether particular advertising and marketing campaigns were effective or not. The overall intuitive feeling was that spending was too high, but there was no empirical data to answer the question of what level of marketing spend was optimal. Transitions executives decided to frame the problem as one of optimizing marketing expenditures and approaches in a way that maximized sales lift for the dollars invested. According to Grady Lenski, who headed Marketing at the time, "We were relying heavily on art to make marketing decisions; we needed more science."

REVIEW OF PREVIOUS FINDINGS. No previous findings on this topic existed; Transitions had customer data that would make such an analysis possible, but it was fragmented across the organization. Lenski and some of his colleagues were aware that it was possible to analyze the effectiveness of different marketing approaches, but didn't know the details.

MODELING (VARIABLE SELECTION). Marketing mix optimization models, which are increasingly employed by large organizations to optimize marketing spending, involve variables of marketing response, marketing costs, and product margins. The optimization models, using linear and nonlinear programming methods, find the weekly or monthly advertising, promotion, and pricing levels that maximize revenue, profit margin, or both. They also determine which particular advertising media are most effective for maximizing these outcomes. They also typically contain a series of "control" variables that might affect consumer spending and purchase behavior, such as weather and macroeconomic data.

DATA COLLECTION. This was one of the most difficult aspects of the analysis for Transitions, since the company works with intermediaries (optical labs, for example) and historically had little contact with or data about end customers. Hence, it couldn't accurately measure whether advertisements were seen by customers or whether they provided any sales lift. Transitions embarked upon a multiyear effort to gather end customer data from its channel partners (some of whom were competitors of its parent companies). Lenski had previously been head of the retail channel, so that facilitated gathering the information. The customer information came into Transitions in thirty different formats, but the company was eventually able to get it into an integrated data warehouse for analysis. Lenski commented that the Marketing organization also needed to persuade different parts of the Transitions organization to provide data. The first time Transitions did the analysis, it did so without a data warehouse.

DATA ANALYSIS. Transitions hired an external consultant to do the data analysis, since it had no one in-house who was familiar with marketing mix optimization models. The analysis initially took several months, since the data had to be gathered and the model involves ruling out a wide variety of other explanatory factors for any marketing response (including weather, competitor marketing, etc.). Now that the models have been developed and refined, they can be finished in a few days.

RESULTS PRESENTATION AND ACTION. Transitions felt that interpreting and presenting the results was important enough to require in-house capabilities, so internal staff were hired to do it. The in-house experts take the model from the consultants and discuss it with executives to determine its implications and combine them with their intuitions about the market. Overall, the results have led to higher spending on marketing for Transitions, particularly for television advertising.

Analytical Thinking Example: *People v. Collins*

People v. Collins was a jury trial in California that made notorious forensic use of mathematics and probability, and it's a good example of how framing the problem incorrectly can lead to a bad outcome.[10] The jury found defendant Malcolm Collins and his wife, Janet Collins, guilty of second-degree robbery. Malcolm appealed the judgment, and the Supreme Court of California eventually set aside the conviction, criticizing the statistical reasoning and disallowing the way the decision was put to the jury. We will examine this case within the six-step framework.

PROBLEM RECOGNITION. Mrs. Juanita Brooks, who had been shopping, was walking home along an alley in the San Pedro area. She was suddenly pushed to the ground by a person whom she couldn't see. She was stunned by the fall and felt some pain. Immediately after the incident, Mrs. Brooks discovered that her purse, containing between $35 and $40, was missing. A witness to the robbery testified that the perpetrators were a black male with a beard and moustache, and a Caucasian female with blonde hair tied in a ponytail. They had escaped in a yellow car. At the seven-day trial, the prosecution experienced some difficulty in establishing the identities of the perpetrators of the crime. The victim could not identify Janet Collins and had never seen her assailant; identification by the witness was incomplete. The prosecutor—perhaps desperate to save the case—decided to help the jury determine the probability that the accused pair fit the description of the witnesses.

REVIEW OF PREVIOUS FINDINGS. It is recognized that the court generally discerns no inherent incompatibility between the disciplines of law and mathematics and intends no disapproval or disparagement of mathematics as a fact-finding process of the law. There have been some criminal cases in which the prosecution used mathematical probability as evidence.

MODELING (VARIABLE SELECTION). The model suggested by the prosecutor is the probability that the accused pair fits the description of the witnesses.

DATA COLLECTION (MEASUREMENT). The prosecutor called to the stand an instructor of mathematics at a state college. Through this witness, he suggested that the jury would be safe in estimating the following probabilities of encountering the attributes of the criminals and crime:

Black man with beard	1 in 10
Man with moustache	1 in 4
White woman with pony tail	1 in 10
White woman with blonde hair	1 in 3
Yellow motor car	1 in 10
Interracial couple in car	1 in 1,000

DATA ANALYSIS. The mathematics instructor suggested that when events are independent, the probabilities of their happening together can be computed by multiplying each probability.

P(A) = the probability that the accused pair fits
the description of the witness

$$= \frac{1}{10} \times \frac{1}{4} \times \frac{1}{10} \times \frac{1}{3} \times \frac{1}{10} \times \frac{1}{1000}$$

$$= \frac{1}{12,000,000}, \text{ or one in 12 million}$$

RESULTS PRESENTATION AND ACTION. The prosecutor arrived at a probability that there was only one chance in 12 million that any couple possessed the distinctive characteristics of the defendants. Accordingly, under this theory, it was to be inferred that there could be but one chance in 12 million that the defendants were innocent. The jury returned a verdict of guilty.

The Collinses appealed this judgment. The California Supreme Court thought that undoubtedly the jurors were unduly impressed by the mystique of the mathematical demonstration but were unable to assess its relevancy or value. The court set aside the conviction, criticizing the statistical reasoning and disallowing the way in which the decision was put to the jury. The Supreme Court pointed out that the specific technique presented through the mathematician's testimony suffered from two important defects. First, the prosecution produced no evidence whatsoever showing the validity of the odds, nor evidence from which such odds could be in any way inferred. Second, there was another glaring defect in the prosecution's technique: an inadequate proof of the statistical independence of the six factors which were brought as evidence by the prosecution (e.g., bearded men commonly sport moustaches).

More importantly, the case and evidence had been framed incorrectly by the prosecutor. Even if the prosecution's conclusion was arithmetically accurate, it could not be concluded that the Collinses were the guilty couple. There was absolutely no guidance on a crucial issue: of the admittedly few such couples that might be encountered in the world, which one, if any, was guilty of committing this robbery?

The relevant variable in this case was not the probability that the accused pair fits the description of the witnesses, but the probability that there are other couples fitting the description of the witnesses, since the accused pair already fit the description. Depending on exactly how many couples there are in the Los Angeles area, the probability of at least one other couple fitting the description might be as high as 40 percent (see the website for this book). Thus the prosecution's computations, far from establishing beyond a reasonable doubt that the Collinses were the couple described by the prosecution's witnesses, imply a very substantial likelihood that the area contained more than one such couple, and that a couple other than the Collinses was the one observed at the scene of the robbery.

After an examination of the entire case, including the evidence, the Supreme Court determined that the judgment against the defendants must therefore be reversed. Bad framing of problems can clearly lead to bad decisions.

3

Solving the Problem

Many people consider this stage—the one in which your quantitative analysis is performed, and your problem "solved"—at least to some degree—as the core of quantitative analysis. It is, of course, a very important activity. But it's a somewhat more structured and better-defined activity than either the problem framing or communications stages that precede and succeed it. If you don't have a lot of mathematical or statistical skills, it may also be the stage that is most likely to be entrusted to others who do have the quantitative abilities you need (see "How to Find a Quant"). But whether or not you're actually crunching the numbers yourself, it's useful to know something about the three steps involved in solving the problem.

A note about the sequence of these three steps may be helpful here. We describe an analytical process that is hypothesis driven. That is, starting with the steps for framing the problem in chapter 2 and continuing with modeling and the selection of variables (the first step in

How to Find a Quant

If you need a quantitative analyst to help you solve your problem, here are some ways to do it:

- If you work for a large company, you probably have some—so look in places like Market Research, Business Intelligence, or Operations Research.

- If you don't have any, there are plenty of consultants to whom you can turn. Do an Internet search for "business analytics consultants" or look at the helpful list from KDnuggets (http://www .kdnuggets.com/companies/consulting.html).

- If you want some offshore analytics consultants, the best are to be found in India; check out such firms as Mu Sigma, Fractal Analytics, and Genpact.

- You may be able to find some quantitative professors or graduate students at your local university; call the department chair's office of the Statistics department, for example.

- If you think you want to hire someone as an employee to do this, there are both websites (the jobs listing site Simply Hired has a number of "quantitative analyst" openings, and analyticrecruiting.com focuses on statisticians, for example) and search firms, such as Smith Hanley Associates, that have recruited such people for decades.

solving the problem, the hypothesis for what is going on in the data is progressively refined. Then the analyst acquires data and solves the problem. Each of these steps is guided by an understanding or at least a guess about how the world works, and then the data analysis step confirms just how correct the understanding or guess really is.

Admittedly, there are some types of analyses in which the process is not driven by a previous hypothesis. In some data-mining and *machine-learning* (in which the software fits models to the data in an automated and rapid fashion to find the best fit) processes, the analyst simply turns the analysis software loose on the data, and it attempts to find patterns. Any hypothesis comes afterward, when the analyst tries to explain and communicate the results.

We're not great fans of this approach, primarily because we think it often leads to inexplicable findings. And because no analyst was trying to use data to confirm his or her understanding of how the world works, no analyst is passionate about explaining the results to others and persuading them to decide differently on the basis of the analysis. However, there are circumstances in which these "black box" approaches to analysis can greatly leverage the time and productivity of human analysts. In big-data environments, where the data just keeps coming in large volumes, it may not always be possible for humans to create hypotheses before sifting through the data. In the context of placing digital ads on publishers' sites, for example, decisions need to be made in thousandths of a second by automated decision systems, and the firms doing this work must generate several thousand statistical models per week. Clearly this type of analysis can't involve a lot of human hypothesizing and reflection on results, and machine learning is absolutely necessary. But for the most part, we'd advise sticking to hypothesis-driven analysis and the steps and sequence in this book.

The Modeling (Variable Selection) Step

A model is a *purposefully simplified representation* of the phenomenon or problem. The word *purposefully* means that the model is built specifically to solve that particular problem. The word *simplified* denotes that we need to leave out all the unnecessary and trivial details and isolate the important, the useful, and the crucial features that make a difference. This kind of variable selection is illustrated as follows:

> A model is to be likened to a caricature. A caricature picks *on* [sic] certain features (a nose, a smile, or a lock of hair) and concentrates on them at the expense of other features. A good caricature is one where these special features have been chosen purposefully and effectively. In the same way a model concentrates on certain features of the real world. Whenever you build a model, you have to be selective. You have to identify those aspects of the real world that are relevant and ignore the rest. You have to create a stripped-down model world which enables you to focus, single-mindedly, on the problem you are trying to solve."[1]

This suggests that models are not exactly correct. In fact, George Box, a famous statistician, once commented that "all models are wrong, but some are useful."[2] The key, of course, is to be able to determine when the model is useful and when it is so wrong that it becomes a major distortion of reality. We'll talk about this issue in chapter 5, but one key factor is determining which variables to include and exclude in the model.

How do you select variables and begin to envision how they might be related to each other? We are still largely in the realm of the subjective here. *Hypotheses*—the early story you tell about your analysis—are simply educated guesses about what variables really matter in your model. At this stage, model building involves using logic, experience, and previous findings to hypothesize your dependent variable—the one you are trying to predict or explain—and the independent variables that will affect it. You will, of course, test your hypothesis

3. Modeling

later; that is what differentiates analytical thinking from less precise approaches to decision making like intuition.

For example, if you are a social scientist trying to predict family income (the dependent variable), you might hypothesize that the independent variables for your model would include age, education, marital status, and the number of full-time employed family members. Those factors make sense only as some that would explain income differentials. Later in the quantitative analysis process (specifically, the data analysis step), you might find out that the model doesn't fit very well, so you might have to go back to the drawing board and think of some new variables on which you could gather data.

Even highly subjective models and variables can be useful in figuring out a problem. For example, Garth Sundem, a pop-science, math, humor, and general geek culture writer, has addressed a variety of life questions through subjective—but still useful—variables.[3] One question he's focused on is whether you should get a pet, and if so, what kind of pet might make sense.

Think about the variables you have to consider in deciding to get a pet. Sundem selected the following variables:

- Need for more love in your life (D) (1–10, with 10 being "day job as prison warden; moonlight for IRS")

- Your general level of responsibility (R) (1–10, with 1 being "confident that taxes, kids, and calendar will sort themselves out if just left alone")

- The largest number of days traveling in the past six months (T)

- Your extra time in hours per day (H)

- Your tolerance for another creature's mischief (M) (1–10, with 1 being Cruella de Vil and 10 being Dr. Doolittle)

- How nurturing you are (N) (1–10, with 1 being "my cactus died")

These are undeniably subjective, but they are also probably use-ful, and also fun. Sundem made up (though it appears very rigorous!) the following equation that yields F_{ido}, the index to decide whether to get a pet:

$$F_{ido} = \frac{(M + N)^{\sqrt{D}} + HR}{8T^2}$$

The most important term of this equation is the need for more love in your life (D), which raises the F_{ido} index. It is also a good sign if you have some extra time (H) to spend with your pet and you are a very re-sponsible person (R). These two variables also interact to increase the F_{ido} index. However, if you travel a lot, your F_{ido} index will fall sub-stantially. Sundem suggests the following pets based on your result:

If F_{ido} is less than 1, sea monkeys would be too ambitious.

If F_{ido} is between 1 and 2, you should get a goldfish.

If F_{ido} is between 2 and 3, you should get a cat.

If F_{ido} is greater than 3, you should get a dog.

Jinho plugged his own numbers in this equation, and his own F_{ido} index (0.7) suggested that even a cactus would be an ambitious pet. One could debate whether this level of quantitative precision is nec-essary in your decision to get a pet or not, but the example does illus-trate that even relatively trivial and highly subjective decisions can be quantified and modeled.

Which variables to throw away and which to keep depends on the purpose of the model and on whether the variable is directly relevant to the solution of the problem. For instance, if you're drawing a map of New York City, the distances between the districts are important and should be proportional to the actual measures. However, if you're drawing a map of the subway lines in New York City, the distances between stations don't need to be proportional to the actual distances; all the subway map needs are the elements that tell how to go from where you are to the station you want to go to.

One great example of the importance of variable selection (and, for that matter, of the review of previous findings) is the controversy over who wrote a series of published letters in 1861. A series of ten letters signed "Quintus Curtius Snodgrass" appeared in the *New Orleans Daily Crescent* that year. In these letters, Mr. Snodgrass [QCS] described his military adventures while serving as a "High Old Private of the Louisiana Guard." The QCS letters, which did not get much attention at that time, were first brought to light in 1934, seventy-three years after their appearance, by author Minnie Brashear in *Mark Twain, Son of Missouri.* In that book, she reprinted one letter and described three others, then argued, "The QCS letters are immensely significant as a link in Mark Twain's development as a humorist; they should be recognized as Twain's; difference in style reflects the fledgling writer's efforts to achieve a more consciously literary manner."[4] The remaining six QCS letters were uncovered by Ernest Leisy and published in 1946.[5] Leisy's careful study of parallels provides the strongest case that the letters were penned by Twain, but other researchers still believed that Mark Twain did not write the QCS letters.

In some previous research findings on whether Shakespeare authored all his works, Thomas Mendenhall published two articles around the turn of the twentieth century, detailing his application of a statistical approach to the authorship controversy. Claude Brinegar, an oil-company executive with strong academic credentials and a hobby of collecting Mark Twain first editions, reviewed previous findings and adopted Mendenhall's method—which has come to be called *stylometry,* or the quantitative analysis of writing style—and applied it to the QCS letters.

This method assumes that every author unconsciously uses words and maintains a similar writing style, at least in the long run.

From a quantitative analysis perspective, this indicates that the proportion of words of various lengths in writing will be maintained across writings. If the proportions of words of various lengths for two sets of writings differ greatly, this should be considered as strong evidence that the two sets were not written by the same person. The variable selection for this analysis, then, basically involved measuring the lengths of words in the QCS letters, and comparing them to works that were definitely written by Twain.

A goodness-of-fit test was conducted to determine whether the same person wrote the two sets of writings. Brinegar's results showed that the discrepancy across the proportions is far too large to be attributed to random fluctuations—that is, the letters do not seem to have been written by Mark Twain (see the website for this book).[6]

We'll say more later in this chapter about the analysis of text (as opposed to numbers), but note that in Brinegar's research, the text was turned into numbers during the analysis process.

Data Collection (Measurement) Step

The next stage is to collect and measure the selected variables. Measuring a variable is assigning a number to the variable; data is just a collection of these numbers. There are various ways to measure variables (see "Ways to Measure Variables"). The recognized problem is first organized through a modeling process into the critical variables, which then become data after measurement. The data you gather, of course, should be driven by the variables you have identified in the previous step.

4. Data collection

Ways to Measure Variables

The three ways to assign measures to variables are:

- **Binary variables:** These have only two values, and for statistical analysis purposes it's often best to measure them as the presence or absence of something with values of 1 and 0. An example could be whether you are male or female (which could be recorded as 0 for no "femaleness," and 1 for being female), or whether you are a US citizen or not.

- **Categorical (also called *nominal*) variables:** These have several possible categories as values, such as eye color, flavors of ice cream, or which state or province you live in. Because they can't easily be converted into numbers where increases or decreases mean anything, there is a special class of statistics for categorical data.

- **Ordinal variables:** These variables have numbers assigned to them, and the higher the number, the more of the variable is present. However, the difference between 1 and 2 may not be the same as the difference between 5 and 6. A typical example of ordinal variables is the *Likert item*—named after the sociologist Rensis Likert—that typically involves survey responses such as strongly disagree, somewhat disagree, neither disagree nor agree, somewhat agree, strongly agree. When several ordinal variables like this are added together, the resulting variable is called a *Likert scale*.

- **Numerical (interval and ratio) variables:** These variables have numbers with standard units, such as weight in pounds or kilograms, or height in inches or centimeters. The higher the number, the more of that variable is present. Numerical variables, then, are well suited to common statistical approaches like correlation and regression analysis.

If the variables you are gathering have been frequently measured and analyzed by others (something that should be revealed in the review of previous findings step), this step will be pretty straightforward for you; you can use someone else's measurement approach. In some cases, however, you'll have to measure variables for the first time. As with the process of selecting variables, even quite subjective things can be measured in systematic ways.

Let's say, for example, that you are a researcher of the popular (judging from television commercials, anyway) topic of erectile dysfunction (ED). It turns out you are in luck; there is a measure that is well accepted in the field. But if you were among the earliest researchers in the field, you'd have to develop your own measure.

In the 1990s R. C. Rosen and his colleagues developed a brief, reliable, self-administered measure of erectile function with the sensitivity and specificity for detecting treatment-related changes in patients with erectile dysfunction.[7] Erectile dysfunction is a self-reported condition, and there are no objective diagnostic tests available to physicians, making it difficult for physicians to make an accurate diagnosis. Rosen and his colleagues determined that the key variables in diagnosing erectile dysfunction were:

Erection confidence

Erection firmness

Maintenance frequency

Maintenance ability

Satisfaction

They measured each variable using the questions shown in table 3-1. In case you're wondering how these questions translate into a diagnosis, they yield possible scores ranging from 5 to 25. ED was classified

TABLE 3-1

Key variables in diagnosing erectile dysfunction

Over the past six months . . .

	Very low / Extremely difficult 1	Low / Very difficult 2	Moderate / Difficult 3	High / Slightly difficult 4	Very high / Not difficult 5
1. How do you rate your confidence that you could get and keep an erection?	Very low 1	Low 2	Moderate 3	High 4	Very high 5
2. When you had erections with sexual stimulation, how often were your erections hard enough for penetration?	Almost never/never 1	A few times (much less than half the time) 2	Sometimes (about half the time) 3	Most times (much more than half the time) 4	Almost always/always 5
3. During intercourse, how often were you able to maintain your erection after penetration?	Almost never/never 1	A few times (much less than half the time) 2	Sometimes (about half the time) 3	Most times (much more than half the time) 4	Almost always/always 5
4. During sexual intercourse, how difficult was it to maintain your erection to completion of intercourse?	Extremely difficult 1	Very difficult 2	Difficult 3	Slightly difficult 4	Not difficult 5
5. When you attempted sexual intercourse, how often was it satisfactory for you?	Almost never/never 1	A few times (much less than half the time) 2	Sometimes (about half the time) 3	Most times (much more than half the time) 4	Almost always/always 5

into five severity levels based on the scores: severe (5–7), moderate (8–11), mild to moderate (12–16), mild (17–21), and none (22–25). This readily self-administered diagnostic tool for ED is called IIEF-5 (the five-item version of the International Index of Erectile Function) and demonstrates how data can be gathered on a subjective topic.

No matter what data you have, there is always the possibility of getting more data, or different data from what you have originally employed in thinking about your problem. Rama Ramakrishnan, the talented quant whom we mentioned in chapter 2, described one way to improve analytical impact in a blog post: "One of my favorites is to get *better data.* Not more data, but data that's *different* from what has been used to solve the problem so far. If you have used demographic data, add purchase data. If you have both, add browsing data. If you have numeric data, add text data (aside: in recent work, we have seen very promising results from complementing traditional retail sales and promotions data with text data for customer modeling and personalization)."[8]

Anand Rajaraman, an expert on data mining, also blogged about the importance of improving analytics by adding new sources of data:

> I teach a class on Data Mining at Stanford. Students in my class are expected to do a project that does some nontrivial data mining. Many students opted to try their hand at the Netflix Challenge: to design a movie recommendations algorithm that does better than the one developed by Netflix.
>
> Here's how the competition works. Netflix has provided a large data set that tells you how nearly half a million people have rated about 18,000 movies. Based on these ratings, you are asked to predict the ratings of these users for movies in the set that they have *not* rated. The first team to beat the accuracy of Netflix's proprietary algorithm by a certain margin wins a prize of $1 million!

Different student teams in my class adopted different approaches to the problem, using both published algorithms and novel ideas. Of these, the results from two of the teams illustrate a broader point. Team A came up with a very sophisticated algorithm using the Netflix data. Team B used a very simple algorithm, but they added in additional data beyond the Netflix set: information about movie genres from the Internet Movie Database (IMDB). Guess which team did better? Team B got much better results, close to the best results on the Netflix leaderboard!![9]

Rajaraman also notes in the same blog post that a new data source—hypertext links—was the primary factor differentiating Google's search algorithm from previous search engine services, which used only the text of the Web pages. In its highly lucrative AdWords advertising algorithm, Google also added some additional data that no one else was using at the time: the click-through rate on each advertiser's ad.

Rajaraman and Ramakrishnan both argue that more and better data beat a better algorithm almost every time. They are referring to online and retail businesses, but there are plenty of other examples where distinctive data has carried the day. Daryl Morey, the general manager of the NBA Houston Rockets, is one of the most analytical managers in professional basketball (we'll describe some of his work in an example in chapter 6). He argues that "real advantage comes from unique data," and employs a number of analysts who classify the defensive moves of opposing players in every NBA game.[10] Morey is also among the NBA's leaders in beginning to analyze the extensive video files recorded in many games. In insurance, one of the factors that has long differentiated Progressive from less analytical auto insurance companies is its distinctive data. It pioneered the use of FICO credit scores (also described in an example in chapter 4) as a variable in insurance pricing models, and has long used more variables and data in analyzing customer risk and pricing than its competitors. Progressive also pioneered the approach of gathering data on how customers drive (with their permission, of course) and pricing insurance based on actual driving behaviors in a program it now calls "Snapshot." You may not want to tell your insurance company how you drive, but if you're a cautious driver, you can get lower rates.

The Value of Secondary Data

Many analysts collect data and then analyze it. But sometimes you can use the data collected by someone else (called *secondary data*). The use of secondary data saves time that would otherwise be spent redundantly collecting the same data. Common sources of secondary data include censuses, surveys, organizational records, and so on. The world is full of it these days, and it's just waiting to be analyzed.

In some cases, secondary data has been used to create very important results. Take, for example, the work of astronomer Johannes Kepler. Although born to a poor family under adverse circumstances, Kepler was lucky enough to acquire very precise secondary data, carefully amassed for several decades, on the motions of objects in the celestial sphere. With his luck and superior mathematical talent, Kepler solved the mystery of the planets.

Kepler's data was primarly gathered by Tycho Brahe (1546–1601), a Danish nobleman and brilliant astronomer who made the most accurate astronomical observations of his time by devising the most precise instruments available prior to the invention of the telescope. With generous royal support from the king of Denmark, Brahe built a research center called Uraniborg (castle of the heavens), which became the finest observatory in Europe. He designed and built new instruments, calibrated them, and instituted scrupulous nightly observations for over twenty years.

In 1600 Brahe invited Kepler—a bright but underprivileged teacher—to become his assistant. Kepler and Brahe did not get along well; their backgrounds and personalities were too different. Brahe feared that his clever young assistant might eclipse him as the premiere astronomer of his day. The next year, in 1601, Brahe suddenly became ill and died. A scramble for Brahe's assets ensued, and Kepler realized that if he didn't act quickly, he would never get to use most of Brahe's data. He immediately took possession of the observations under his care (in his own expression, "usurping" them) and retained control of them. Two days after Brahe's funeral, Kepler was appointed as Brahe's successor to the post of imperial mathematician. Now Brahe's incomparable collection of astronomical observations was in Kepler's hands. Utilizing the data, Kepler was eventually able to find that the orbits of the planets were ellipses, and formulated his three laws of planetary motion.[11]

Of course, there are many examples of using secondary data that are much more contemporary. Take, for example, the company Recorded Future. Its source of secondary data is a familiar one—the Internet. Recorded Future, founded by analytics expert Christopher Ahlberg, analyzes the Internet to count and classify how often entities and events are mentioned. The company has a particular focus on counting predictions—mentions of the future. It sells its data and analyses to government intelligence agencies, which have an obvious interest in how often things like terrorism or war are being mentioned, and financial services firms, which are interested in words that indicate investor and consumer sentiments.

Primary Data

However, if you're not lucky enough, as Kepler or Recorded Future were, to inherit such valuable secondary data or when data directly relevant to your problem is not available, the variables must be measured by the researcher (*primary data*). There are several types of measures: a survey includes the design and implementation of interviews or questionnaires; observational techniques involve someone's making observations, directly or unobtrusively; carefully designed and controlled mad scientist experiments can be used for specific problems. Which method you use in your study depends on the characteristics of both the recognized problem and the variables selected.

STRUCTURED AND UNSTRUCTURED DATA. For centuries, almost all quantitative analysis was performed on *structured* data—that is, data in numeric form that could easily be put into rows and columns. Whether the analysis was done with a spreadsheet, a powerful statistical package, or a handheld calculator, rows and columns (with rows typically representing the cases or observations, and each variable shown in a column) were the way data was structured. About the only question you had to ask was how big the numbers could get and how many decimal places should be represented.

That all began to change with the advent of textual analysis in the latter years of the twentieth century. As we described in the example of Mark Twain's letters, researchers began to look for patterns in text as well as numbers. How often did certain words occur was a typical question. Text is an example of *unstructured data*—because it usually comes in a continuous stream, it is hard to put into neat rows and columns.

However, it was after 2000 that unstructured data really began to explode in volume and variety. That year marked the beginning of widespread use of the Internet, which led to massive volumes of text, images, and clickstreams to be analyzed by organizations like Recorded Future. Telecommunications and social media contributed large volumes of social network–oriented data. The volume of audio and video data that organizations wanted to analyze also experienced geometrical growth around this time. The genetic revolution led to large volumes of genetic and proteomic data.

Now we're officially in the era of big data, in which organizations routinely deal with multiple petabytes (1,000 terabytes, or 10^{15} bytes—that's 1,000,000,000,000,000 pieces of information) of data. eBay, for example, has a data warehouse comprising more than forty petabytes. Every time you click on a used camera or a flowered vase, your activity adds to the total.

Analysis of this data is often very different from that of structured numerical data in the initial stages. In many cases, we have to do a lot of data filtering, classification, and other forms of preparation before we can even count the data. The definition of a *data scientist* is someone who is an expert not only at analyzing data, but at getting it in shape to analyze. Tools like Hadoop and MapReduce, which many organizations working with big data are beginning to employ, are intended to filter and classify data so that it can be analyzed quantitatively. Video and voice data also requires substantial preparation before it can be analyzed with quantitative methods. In many cases, after that the organization will analyze the data with traditional statistical software. As Bill Franks of Teradata points out in an International Institute for Analytics blog post:[12]

> Unstructured data has been a very popular topic lately since so many big data sources are unstructured. However, an important nuance is often missed—the fact is that virtually no analytics directly analyze unstructured data. Unstructured data may be an input to an analytic process, but when it comes time to do any actual analysis, the unstructured data itself isn't utilized. "How can that be?" you ask. Let me explain . . .
>
> Let's start with the example of fingerprint matching. If you watch shows like CSI, you see them match up fingerprints all

the time. A fingerprint image is totally unstructured and also can be fairly large in size if the image is of high quality. So, when police on TV or in real life go to match fingerprints, do they match up actual images to find a match? No. What they do is first identify a set of important points on each print. Then, a map or polygon is created from those points. It is the map or polygon created from the prints that is actually matched. More important is the fact that the map or polygon is fully structured and small in size, even though the original prints were not. While unstructured prints are an input to the process, the actual analysis to match them up doesn't use the unstructured images, but rather structured information extracted from them.

An example everyone will appreciate is the analysis of text. Let's consider the now popular approach of social media sentiment analysis. Are tweets, Facebook postings, and other social comments directly analyzed to determine their sentiment? Not really. The text is parsed into words or phrases. Then, those words and phrases are flagged as good or bad. In a simple example, perhaps a "good" word gets a 1, a "bad" word gets a –1, and a "neutral" word gets a 0. The sentiment of the posting is determined by the sum of the individual word or phrase scores. Therefore, the sentiment score itself is created from fully structured numeric data that was derived from the initially unstructured source text. Any further analysis on trends or patterns in sentiment is based fully on the structured, numeric summaries of the text, not the text itself.

Similar to Franks's examples above, many big-data applications are initially focused on unstructured data, but after they are processed by such tools as Hadoop and MapReduce, they are able to be analyzed as structured data using standard visual analytics or statistical software.

Data Analysis Step

Since data itself does not tell us anything, we need to analyze it in order to decipher its meaning and relationships. Data analysis entails finding consistent patterns; in other words, the relationships among the variables that are embedded in the data. When you see patterns emerge, numbers become easier to explain. When you extract these patterns from the variables, the problem becomes easier to solve. For instance, let's assume that we collected data, through a telephone survey of a sample of voters, for presidential candidates. By analyzing the data, we try to find the patterns for which *region*, *education*, *income*, *gender*, *age*, and *party affiliation* indicate probable support for any particular candidate. In finding patterns in data, various techniques—from basic analyses such as graphs, percentages, and means, to more elaborate statistical methods—can be used. The characteristics and complexity decide specifically which techniques should be implemented.

Think back to the different types of analytical stories we described in chapter 2. If you're just telling a "here's what happened" story, then the only type of analysis you are going to do is probably some form of reporting; that is, you're going to create a report or a set of graphics saying how many things in what category were found in your data. At most you'll report some *measures of central tendency*, such as means or medians. For that approach, you will need software that focuses primarily on reporting. Dashboards, scorecards, and alerts are all forms of reporting. In "Key Software Vendors for Different Analysis Types," we list some of the key vendors for reporting software.

5. Data analysis

Key Software Vendors for Different Analysis Types (listed alphabetically)

REPORTING SOFTWARE

- BOARD International

- IBM Cognos

- Information Builders WebFOCUS

- Oracle Business Intelligence (including Hyperion)

- Microsoft Excel/SQL Server/SharePoint

- MicroStrategy

- Panorama

- SAP BusinessObjects

INTERACTIVE VISUAL ANALYTICS

- QlikTech QlikView

- Tableau

- TIBCO Spotfire

QUANTITATIVE OR STATISTICAL MODELING

- IBM SPSS

- R (an open-source software package)

- SAS

While all of the listed reporting software vendors also have capabilities for graphical display, some vendors focus specifically on *interactive visual analytics*, or the use of visual representations of data and reporting. Such tools are often used simply to graph data and for *data discovery*—understanding the distribution of the data, identifying *outliers* (data points with unexpected values) and visual relationships between variables. So we've listed these as a separate category.

We've also listed key vendors of software for the other category of analysis, which we'll call *quantitative* or *statistical modeling*. In that category, you're trying to use statistics to understand the relationships between variables and to make inferences from your sample to a larger population. Predictive analytics, randomized testing, and the various forms of regression analysis are all forms of this type of modeling. The software vendors for this type of data tend to be different from the reporting software vendors, though the two categories are blending a bit over time.

Microsoft Excel, for example, perhaps the most widely used analytical software tool in the world (though most people think of it as a spreadsheet tool), can do some statistical analysis (and visual analytics) as well as reporting, but it's not the most robust statistical software if you have a lot of data or a complex statistical model to build, so it's not listed in that category. Excel's usage for analytics in the corporate environment is frequently augmented by other Microsoft products, including SQL Server (primarily a database tool with some analytical functionality) and SharePoint (primarily a collaboration tool, with some analytical functionality).

Types of Models

There are a variety of model types that analysts and their organizations use to think analytically and make data-based decisions. It's not really part of the subject of this book to get into teaching you statistics, but it's useful to know the criteria that quantitative analysts use to determine what type of model to employ. We believe this material enables readers to jump-start and firmly grasp the cores of analytics.

If we want to understand the types of models that would work in a situation, we first need to outline specifics about the situation faced by decision makers (or their analysts). There are three questions we need to think about to identify the appropriate model:

- How many variables are to be analyzed at the same time? The possibilities for analysis are one variable (*univariate model*), two variables (*bivariate*), and three or more variables (*multivariate*). That about covers all the options.

- Do we want description or inference questions answered? *Descriptive statistics* simply describe the data that you have and don't try to generalize beyond it. Means, medians, and standard deviations are examples of descriptive statistics. They are often useful, but not very interesting from a statistical or mathematical perspective. *Inferential statistics* take a sample of data and try to infer or generalize the findings to a broader population. Correlation and regression analyses (see below) are examples of inferential statistics, because they incorporate an estimate of how likely the relationships observed in the sample would hold up in a broader population. Statisticians and quantitative analysts get much more excited about inferential statistics than descriptive ones.

- What level of measurement is available in the variable(s) of interest? This is described in "Ways to Measure Variables" earlier.

The specific type of model you (or your quantitative helpers) employ is going to be driven by the kind of story you are trying to tell and the type of data you have. Some sample attributes of stories and data—and the types of models that result from them—are described next. They don't represent all of the possible variations in model types, but they probably describe about 90 percent of what organizations do with analytics day to day.

- *Two numerical data variables:* If you are only trying to relate a couple of things that can be measured numerically, you will probably want to use some type of *correlation analysis*. This is one of the simplest statistical analyses you can perform. Basically it assesses whether two variables—take the weight and height of a series of people, for example—vary together. Does weight go up as height goes up? Yes, it generally does, so weight and height are said to be highly correlated. Because correlation is an inferential statistic, there are also tests to determine whether a certain level of correlation is likely to have occurred by chance. If you hear that a correlation is "significant at the .05 significance level," for example, it means that in only five cases out of one hundred would that relationship in your sample have occurred by chance in the broader population.

- *Two or a few categorical variables:* If you're using survey data and your data come in *nominal categories* (for example, male or female gender, or young/middle/old age), you will want to use a series of techniques for categorical data analysis. The outputs of this sort of analysis are often displayed in tables, with the numbers of observations in the cells of the table. For example, if you're relating gender to age, you might find relatively equal numbers of men and women in the young and middle-age categories, but since women generally live a bit longer than men, you might find more women in the old-age cells. If that or some other pattern is pronounced in your data, your analysis might conclude that your data table shows a significant (not likely to be based on chance) relationship according to a chi square (goodness-of-fit) test. Again, the relationship might be significant at the .05 or .01 significance

level. Binary categorical variables like gender can also be han-
dled with regression analysis (see below) using "dummy" variables, or those that can be coded as 0 for the absence of a
factor (e.g., "maleness"), and 1 for the presence of it.

- *More than two numerical data variables:* Extending correlation
  analysis beyond two variables with numerical variables is
  called *regression analysis*—sometimes *multiple regression* (because you are using multiple variables to explain the value of
  another variable) or *linear regression* (because the relationships between the variables stays similar throughout the
  ranges of the variables). Regression is an approach to fitting an
  equation (or a line in graphical terms) to a distribution of data
  gathered in the past, but once you have a good model, you can
  use it to predict the future. A regression model assigns coefficients to each variable that is explaining or predicting the
  value of another variable.

For an example of a multiple linear regression, let's look at the way
Orley Ashenfelter, an economist at Princeton, has used regression
analysis to find out what predicts the auction prices of valuable
French wines. His prediction of wine prices based on vintage
growing-season weather produced consternation among the wine
experts, and even incensed them. (The *New York Times* published a
front-page article about his prediction entitled "Wine Equation Puts
Some Noses Out of Joint."[13]) If you have a good equation, who needs
experts?

Most observers at least agree that good wine is produced when the
previous winter has been wet, the growing season is warm, and harvest season is dry. Thus, for the weather variables that affect the
quality of a vintage, Ashenfelter selected three independent variables: average growing season temperature, harvest rainfall, and

winter rainfall. In addition, since wines usually taste better with age, the age of the vintage is used as an independent variable.

The quality of the vintage is reflected in the prices of mature wine, which became the dependent variable that Ashenfelter tried to predict. The prices in the London auction market for six Bordeaux Chateaux from 1960 to 1969 were collected. The vintages from 1960 to 1969 were selected because these wines were fully matured and there was little remaining uncertainty about their quality. The measures for the weather variables were obtained from the grower's local weather agency.

Ashenfelter conducted a regression of the (logarithm) price of the vintage on the age of the vintage and the weather variables. He obtained the following wine equation:

Wine quality = 12.145 (a constant) + .0238 vintage age + 0.616 average growing season temperature − 0.00386 harvest rainfall + 0.00117 winter rainfall

As the signs of the coefficients indicate, vintage age, moderate growing season temperature, and winter rainfall have direct, positive effects on wine quality. Harvest rainfall is negatively associated with wine quality. The *R-square* (see more on this next) of the equation was 0.828, which reveals that these variables explain 83 percent of the variation in the vintage prices. In short, information on these variables alone plays a very big role in price determination. One can see why the experts might have found the results somewhat challenging and less interesting than talking about *terroir*, oak barrels, and overripened fruit.

In "Key Statistical Concepts and Techniques," we describe the commonly used inferential statistics models (as we noted, the descriptive and reporting-oriented ones are useful, but not very interesting in a quantitative sense). There are, of course, whole books on this topic, so this is only a brief introduction.

Key Statistical Concepts and Techniques[a]

ANOVA: Analysis of variance; a statistical test of whether the means of more than two groups are all equal.

Causality: The relationship between an event (the cause) and a second event (the effect), where the second event is understood as a consequence of the first. In common usage, causality is also the relationship between a set of factors (causes) and a phenomenon (the effect). Three conditions of causality are:

- A cause must precede its effect in time and space.

- A cause must be present when its effect reacts.

- A cause must be absent when its effect is nonreactive.

Clustering or cluster analysis: Assigning observations (e.g., records in a database) into groups (called *clusters*) so that objects within clusters are similar in some manner while objects across clusters are dissimilar to each other. Clustering is a main task of exploratory data mining, and a common technique for statistical data analysis used in many fields.

Correlation: The extent to which two or more variables are related to one another. The degree of relatedness is expressed as a correlation coefficient, which ranges from -1.0 to $+1.0$.

Correlation = $+1$ (Perfect positive correlation, meaning that both variables always move in the same direction together)

Correlation = 0 (No relationship between the variables)

Correlation = -1 (Perfect negative correlation, meaning that as one variable goes up, the other always trends downward)

Correlation does not imply causation. Correlation is a necessary but insufficient condition for casual conclusions.

Dependent variable: The variable whose value is unknown that you would like to predict or explain. For example, if you wish to predict the quality of a vintage wine using average growing season temperature, harvest rainfall, winter rainfall, and the age of the vintage, the quality of a vintage wine would be the dependent variable. Alternative names are *explained variable* and *response variable*.

Factor analysis: A statistical procedure that takes a large number of variables or objects and uncovers the underlying relationships among them. This allows numerous interrelated variables to be condensed into fewer dimensions, called factors. This is often used for data reduction and/or structure identification. For example, if a researcher has over one hundred variables of interest to study, a factor analysis might enable a composite metric to be created that would capture the essence of the hundred variables in only a handful of composite measures or factors.

Chi square (goodness-of-fit) test: A statistical test that determines how well sample data fits a specified type of distribution. Measures of goodness of fit typically summarize the discrepancy between observed values and the values expected under the specified distribution. The most frequently used goodness-of-fit test is to check whether outcome frequencies follow a specified distribution.

Hypothesis testing: A systematic approach to assessing a tentative belief (claim) about reality. It involves confronting the belief or claim with evidence and deciding, in light of this evidence, whether the belief can be maintained as reasonable or must be discarded as untenable. This claim is divided into two competing hypotheses: the null and alternative hypotheses. The *null hypothesis* (H_0) suggests that there is no statistically significant difference or relationship between a given set of observations. The *alternative hypothesis* (H_a or H_1) suggests that the change or relationship we wish to show does exist in the data. Hypothesis testing involves comparing empirically observed sample findings with theoretically expected findings—that is, expected if the null hypothesis is true. For example, if you wish to predict the quality of a vintage wine using the age of the vintage, a null hypothesis could be "The age of the vintage is not a significant predictor of wine quality," while the alternative hypothesis might be "The age of the vintage is a significant predictor of wine quality." Data is collected and tested to see how "unusual" it is under the temporary assumption that H_0 is true. Rare or unusual data (often represented by a *p-value* below a specified threshold) is an indication that H_0 is false, which constitutes a *statistically significant* result and support of the alternative hypothesis.

Independent variable: A variable whose value is known and used to help predict or explain a dependent variable. For example, if you wish to predict the quality of a vintage wine using various predictors (average growing season temperature, harvest rainfall, winter rainfall, and the age of the vintage), the various predictors would serve as independent variables. Alternative names are *explanatory variable*, *predictor variable*, and *regressor*.

***p*-value:** When performing a hypothesis test, the *p*-value gives the probability of data occurrence under the assumption that H_0 is true. Small p-values are an indication of rare or unusual data from H_0, which in turn provides support that H_0 is actually false (and thus support of the alternative hypothesis). In hypothesis testing, we "reject the null hypothesis" when the p-value is less than the significance level α (Greek alpha), which is often 0.05 or 0.01. When the null hypothesis is rejected, the result is said to be statistically significant.

Regression: Any statistical method that seeks to establish an equation that allows the unknown value of one dependent variable to be estimated from the known value of one or more independent variables. *Simple regression* uses one independent variable to predict a dependent variable. *Multiple regression* uses multiple independent variables to predict a dependent variable. *Logistic regression* uses multiple independent variables to predict a binary, categorical dependent variable (e.g., yes/no, purchase/no purchase, pros/cons).

R-squared (R^2): The most popular measure of how well an estimated regression line fits the sample data on which it is based. It also indicates the amount of variability of the dependent variable accounted for by the regression line. It's a proportion ranging between 0 and 1, and if, for example, it's .52, it means that 52% of the variance in the dependent variable is explained by the independent variables used in the regression. In general, the higher the value is, the better the model.

Significance level or alpha/α: Among all the sample results that are possible when the null hypothesis is true, the (arbitrary) maximum proportion of these results that is considered sufficiently unusual to reject the null hypothesis is called the significance level.

In other words, the significance level indicates the amount of evidence required to accept that an event is unlikely to have arisen by chance (and thus contradicts H_0). The traditional level of significance is 5 percent (0.05); however, stricter values can be used for situations that demand stronger evidence before the alternative hypothesis is accepted (e.g., $\alpha = 1$ percent [0.01]). A value of 5 percent signifies that we need data that occurs less than 5 percent of the time from H_0 (if H_0 were indeed true) for us to doubt H_0 and reject it as being true. In practice, this is often assessed by calculating a *p*-value; *p*-values less than alpha are indication that H_0 is rejected and the alternative supported.

t-test or student's t-test: A test statistic that tests whether the means of two groups are equal, or whether the mean of one group has a specified value.

Type I error or α error: This error occurs when the null hypothesis is true, but it is rejected. In traditional hypothesis testing, one rejects the null hypothesis if the *p*-value is smaller than the significance level α. So, the probability of incorrectly rejecting a true null hypothesis equals α and thus this error is also called α error.

a. For the descriptions in this section, we've referred to the pertinent definitions in *Wikipedia*, Heinz Kohler's *Statistics for Business and Economics* (2002), and Dell's *Analytics Cheat Sheet* (2012, Tables 6 and 8).

Changing the Model

As you might guess, no model lasts forever. If the world has changed in some critical aspect, chances are good that the model is no longer an adequate representation of the world. We'll describe the importance of assumptions within models—and surfacing them so that all involved can know whether they still apply—later in this book. Suffice it to say here that any organization or individual involved with quantitative models should regularly review them to ensure that they still make sense and still fit the data—and if not, change them. By *regularly*, we mean at least every year or so, unless there is reason to examine them more quickly.

In some settings, models need to be changed much more frequently. For example, if you're basing financial trades on the model, you probably need to examine them very often. James Simons, the proprietor of Renaissance Technologies, runs one of the world's largest hedge funds and changes his models all the time. He hires professors, code breakers, and statistically minded scientists and engineers. Since its inception in March 1988, Simons's flagship $3.3 billion Medallion Fund, which traded everything from soybean futures to French government bonds, has amassed annual returns of 35.6 percent. For the eleven full years ending December 1999, Medallion's cumulative returns were an eye-popping 2,478.6 percent. Simons earned an estimated $2.5 billion in 2008 and, with an estimated net worth of $8.7 billion, he is ranked by *Forbes* as the eightieth-richest person in the world and the twenty-ninth-richest person in America. He was named by the *Financial Times* in 2006 as "the world's smartest billionaire."[14]

Simons acknowledges that trading opportunities are, by their nature, small and fleeting. He put it at one seminar like this: "Efficient market theory is correct in that there are no gross inefficiencies. But we look at anomalies that may be small in size and brief in time. We make our forecast. Shortly thereafter, we reevaluate the situation and revise our forecast and our portfolio. We do this all day long. We're always in and out and out and in. So we're dependent on activity to make money."

To stay ahead of the pack, Simons changes his models weekly. Things change, and being able to adjust is what has made Mr. Simons so successful. He says: "Statistic predictor signals erode over the next several years; it can be five years or ten years. You have to keep coming up with new things because the market is against us. If you don't keep getting better, you're going to do worse."

Analytical Thinking Example: Black-Scholes Option Pricing Model

Fischer Black and Myron Scholes solved a problem in stock valuations that had long bedeviled investors.[15] Black, a PhD in applied mathematics from Harvard, was then working at the consulting firm of Arthur D. Little, Inc.; Scholes, a freshly minted PhD in economics from Chicago, had just joined the faculty of the MIT Finance Department.

There is a lot of specialized terminology in options pricing. An *option* is a security giving the right, but not the obligation, to buy or sell an asset, subject to certain conditions, within a specified period of time. The price that is paid for the asset when the option is exercised is called the *exercise price*. The last day on which the option may be exercised is called the *maturity date*. The simplest kind of option, which is often referred to as a *call option*, is one that gives the right to buy a single share of common stock. A *risk premium* is the amount an investor pays for a stock or other asset over the price of a risk-free investment.

In general, the higher the price of the stock, the greater the value of the option. When the stock price is much greater than the exercise price, the option is almost sure to be exercised. On the other hand, if the price of the stock is much less than the exercise price, the option is almost sure to expire without being exercised, so its value will be near zero. If the expiration date of the option is very far in the future, the value of the option will be approximately equal to the price of the stock. Normally, the value of an option declines as its maturity date approaches, as long as the value of the stock does not change. However, the amount to pay for a risk premium is uncertain.

PROBLEM RECOGNITION AND FRAMING. A prerequisite for efficient management of risk of options and other derivative securities is that such instruments are correctly valued, or priced. Previous attempts to value derivatives were flawed in several ways; a new method, theoretically rigorous and empirically sound, to determine the value of derivatives was needed.

REVIEW OF PREVIOUS FINDINGS.   Attempts to value derivatives have a long history, dating as far back as 1900. Most of the previous work on the valuation of options has been expressed in terms of warrants (call options issued by firms that give the holder the right to purchase shares at a specified price from the firm), all producing valuation formulas of the same general type. These, however, were not complete, since they all involve one or more arbitrary parameters and suffer from a fundamental shortcoming: risk premiums were not dealt with properly. Unfortunately, there seemed to be no model of the pricing of securities under the condition of capital market equilibrium that would make this an appropriate procedure for determining the value of a warrant. Black and Scholes, for the first time in history, tried to derive a theoretical valuation formula using this equilibrium condition.

MODELING (VARIABLE SELECTION).   Five variables were determined to be affecting the valuation of options, as follows:

Time to maturity

Spot price of the underlying asset

Exercise price

Risk-free interest rate

Volatility of returns of the underlying asset

Note that an investor's attitude toward risk was not included. Black and Scholes made a vital contribution by showing that it is in fact not necessary to use any risk premium when valuing an option. This does not mean that the risk premium disappears; instead it is already included in the stock price.

DATA COLLECTION (MEASUREMENT). Black and Scholes's model is derived from some technical assumptions and the presumed relationships between the variables. No measurement was made in the developmental stage of the model. However, Black and Scholes performed empirical tests of their theoretically derived model on a large body of call-option data in their paper "The Pricing of Options and Corporate Liabilities."[16]

DATA ANALYSIS.   Black and Scholes could derive a partial differential equation based on some arguments and technical assumptions (a model from calculus, not statistics). The solution to this equation was the Black-Scholes formula, which suggested how the price of a call option might be calculated as a function of a risk-free interest rate, the price variance of the asset on which the option was written, and the parameters of the option (strike price, term, and the market price of the underlying asset). The formula introduces the concept that, the higher the share price today, the higher the volatility of the share price, the higher the risk-free interest rate, the longer the time to maturity, and the lower the exercise price, then the higher the option value. The valuation of other derivative securities proceeds along similar lines.

RESULTS PRESENTATION AND ACTION.   Black and Scholes tried to publish their paper first by submitting it to the *Journal of Political Economy*, but it was promptly rejected. Still convinced that their paper had merit, they submitted it to the *Review of Economics and Statistics*, where it received the same treatment. The thought that the valuation of an option can be mathematically solved without incorporating an investor's attitude toward risk then seemed unfamiliar and inadmissible to most reviewers. After making revisions based on extensive comments from several famous economists, they resubmitted it to the *Journal of Political Economy* and finally were able to publish it. Subsequently, Robert Merton, then a professor at MIT, published a paper expanding the mathematical understanding of the Black-Scholes model.

Despite the issues with getting the work published, thousands of traders and investors now use this formula every day to value stock options in markets throughout the world. It is easy to calculate and explicitly models the relationships among all the variables. It is a useful approximation, particularly when analyzing the directionality that prices move when crossing critical points. Even when the results are not completely accurate, they serve as a sound first approximation to which adjustments can later be made.

Black and Scholes's model has become indispensable not only in option pricing but also in the analysis of many economic problems. It has become the most successful theory in the whole economics discipline. Merton and Scholes received the 1997 Nobel Prize in Economics for developing a new method to determine the value of derivatives. Though ineligible for the prize because he had died in 1995, Black was mentioned as a contributor by the Swedish academy.

Analytical Thinking Example: The Suspicious Husband

In 1973, the following item appeared in the "Dear Abby" newspaper advice column:[17]

> *Dear Abby: You wrote in your column that a woman is pregnant for 266 days. Who said so? I carried my baby for ten*

months and five days, and there is no doubt about it because I know the exact date my baby was conceived. My husband is in the Navy and it couldn't have possibly been conceived any other time because I saw him only once for an hour, and I didn't see him again until the day before the baby was born. I don't drink or run around, and there is no way this baby isn't his, so please print a retraction about that 266-day carrying time because otherwise I am in a lot of trouble.

—San Diego Reader

Abby's answer was somewhat reassuring, but not very quantitative:

Dear Reader: The average gestation period is 266 days. Some babies come early. Others come late. Yours was late.

If Abby had been more quantitative, she would have written a response to "San Diego Reader" with more numbers. Bringing numbers always turns out to be more persuasive, and this is a relatively simple problem involving probability. Let's present this problem within the six-step framework.

PROBLEM RECOGNITION.   The question here is not whether the baby was late; that fact is already known. Ten months and five days is approximately 310 days—well over the 266 that Abby correctly suggests is average. The question is, what is the probability of this case (or how unusual is it)? Is it unusual enough to suggest that the woman is not telling the truth?

REVIEW OF PREVIOUS FINDINGS.   We can safely assume that the distribution of gestation period is roughly normal (that is, it follows a bell-shaped curve). The probability that a pregnancy would last at least 310 days can be easily calculated from the *Z-score* (the number of standard deviations from the mean) of the standard normal distribution, the basics of elementary statistics.

MODELING (VARIABLE SELECTION).   The probability that a pregnancy would last at least 310 days.

DATA COLLECTION (MEASUREMENT).   Current data suggest that the actual mean gestation period is 266 days with a standard deviation of 16 days.

DATA ANALYSIS.   When the mean length of pregnancies is 266 days with a standard deviation of 16 days, the likelihood that a pregnancy would last at least 10 months and 5 days (300 days or longer) is 0.003, based on a normal distribution.

RESULTS PRESENTATION AND ACTION.   This indicates that three babies out of a thousand are born this late. This sounds very small, but not when you apply it to large numbers. Since about 4 million babies are born each year in America, there are approximately twelve thousand babies born this late. Abby could have answered like this: "There are about twelve thousand babies born this late each year in the United States. Yours is just one of them." This response would not only have been reassuring to the wife but persuasive to her husband as well.

In statistical hypothesis testing, the probability of 0.003 calculated above is called the p-value—the probability of obtaining a test statistic (e.g., Z-value of 2.75 in this case) at least as extreme as the one that was actually observed (a pregnancy that would last at least ten months and five days), assuming that the null hypothesis is true. In this example the null hypothesis (H_0) is "This baby is my husband's." In traditional hypothesis testing, one rejects the null hypothesis if the p-value is smaller than the significance level. In this case a p-value of 0.003 would result in the rejection of the null hypothesis even at the 1 percent significance level—typically the lowest level anyone uses. Normally, then, we reject the null hypothesis that this baby is the San Diego Reader's husband's baby. How can we interpret this (wrong) test result? This is a typical example of a type I error (or α error), the wrong decision that is made when a test rejects a true null hypothesis (H_0). In other words, sometimes life falls outside of the predictions of probability theory.

4

Communicating and
Acting on Results

Communicating the results of your analysis to stakeholders is the final stage in our three-stage, six-step framework, and it's extremely important. Even if you've performed the other steps brilliantly,

6. Results presentation and action

nothing good happens unless this step is done well. Analysts who care whether their work is implemented—whether it changes decisions and influences actions—care a lot about this stage and devote a lot of time and effort to it. Analysts who don't care about such things—who are, in our view, bad analysts—believe that the results "speak for themselves," and don't worry much about this stage.

This has also not historically been viewed as a fit subject for formal education. Academics—particularly those with a strong analytical orientation in their own research and teaching—have traditionally been far too focused on the analytical methods themselves and not enough on how to communicate them effectively. Fortunately, this situation is beginning to change. Xiao-Li Meng, the chair of the Harvard Statistics Department (recently named the Dean of the Graduate School of Arts and Sciences at Harvard) has described his goal of creating "effective statistical communicators":

> In recent years we have taken a broader view of statistical education for Harvard's undergraduates, by shifting the focus from preparing a few to pursue Ph.D. level quantitative studies to helping many gain a basic appreciation of statistical argument and insight, as a part of their liberal arts critical thinking training and experience. Intriguingly, the journey, guided by the philosophy that one can become a wine connoisseur without ever knowing how to make wine, apparently has led us to produce many more future winemakers than when we focused only on producing a vintage.[1]

Using this philosophy, Meng and his colleagues developed a course for undergraduates called Real-Life Statistics: Your Chance for Happiness (or Misery). It includes modules on statistical views of such topics as "Romance," "Wine and Chocolate," "Finance," "Medical" (including clinical trials of Viagra), and "Stock Market." Meng is trying to make statistics "not just palatable, but delicious!"[2]

You can use the information in this chapter whether you are an analyst or a consumer of analytics (put another way, an analytical winemaker or a consumer of wine). Analysts, of course, can make their research outputs more interesting and attention-getting so as to inspire more action. Consumers of analytics—say, managers who have commissioned an analytical project—should insist that they receive results in interesting, comprehensible formats. If the audience for a quantitative analysis is bored or confused, it's probably not their fault. Consumers of analytics can work with quantitative analysts to try to make results more easily understood and used. And of course, it's generally the consumers of analytics that make decisions and take action on the results.

The essence of this stage is describing the problem and the story behind it, the model, the data employed, and the relationships among the variables in the analysis. When those relationships are identified, their meaning should be interpreted, stated, and presented relevant to the problem. The clearer the results presentation, the more likely that the quantitative analysis will lead to decisions and actions—which are, after all, usually the point of doing the analysis in the first place.

The presentation of the results needs to cover the outline of the research process, the summary of the results, and the recommendation for solving the problem—though probably not in that order. It's usually best to start with the summary and recommendations. The best ways to present the results are either to convene a meeting with the relevant people and present them with a Q&A session or write a formal report. If the problem and the results have some academic significance, you may write an article and try to publish it within the related discipline.

As we noted in chapter 2, presenting data in the form of black-and-white numeric tables is a pretty good way to have your results ignored—even if it's a simple "here's what happened" analytical story. This type of story can almost always be described in simple graphical terms—a bar chart, pie chart, graph, or something more visually ambitious, such as an interactive display. There are some people who prefer rows and columns of numbers over more visually stimulating presentations of data, but there aren't many of them. If you can use color and movement to liven up the presentation in ways that add to the clarity of the results, so much the better.

Telling a Story with Data

The most successful analysts are those who can "tell a story with data." We've discussed several different types of stories that can be told with analytics in chapter 2. But regardless of the type of story and the means of getting it across, the elements of all good analytical stories are similar. They have a strong narrative, typically driven by the business problem or objective. A presentation of an analytical story on customer loyalty might begin, "As you all know, we have wanted for a long time to identify our most loyal customers and ways to make them even more loyal to us—and now we can do it."

Good stories present findings in terms that the audience can understand. If the audience is highly quantitative and technical, then statistical or mathematical terms—even an occasional equation—can be used. Most frequently, however, the audience will not be technical, so the findings should be presented in terms of concepts that the audience can understand and identify with. In business, this often takes the form of money earned or saved, or return on investment.

Good stories conclude with actions to take and the predicted consequences of those actions. Of course, that means that analysts need to consult with key stakeholders in advance to discuss various action scenarios. No one wants to be told by a quantitative analyst, "You need to do this, and you need to do that."

David Schmitt, the head of an analytical group at IHG (Interconti-nental Hotels Group), a global hotel chain, believes strongly in the importance of analytical storytelling, and has blogged about some of the attributes of a great story:[3]

> So what makes a good story? Whenever possible, I turn to the experts, and these days the very best storytellers are at Pixar, home of such great stories as *Finding Nemo, The Incredibles,* and, of course, *Toy Story.* Emma Coats, a storyboard artist at Pixar, published on Twitter a list of twenty-two rules for storytelling. Although all twenty-two may not directly apply to analytics, I find these three particularly relevant:
>
> - "Come up with your ending before you figure out your mid-dle. Seriously. Endings are hard, get yours working up front": The conclusion of your analysis is the only reason why you are telling the story. When you finish, what do you want your audience to know? More importantly, what do you want them to do? Use this as a test for every other part of your story, and only keep those things that support your ending.
>
> - "Putting it on paper lets you start fixing it. If it stays in your head, a perfect idea, you'll never share it with anyone": Cre-ative storytelling may begin in your head, but when you put it on paper, the story will take you places you may not have even considered. I can get wrapped around the axle think-ing and rethinking a presentation in my head, but once I force myself to write it down (paper, Word, or PowerPoint— it doesn't matter!) the creative juices really start to flow.
>
> - "What's the essence of your story? Most economical telling of it? If you know that, you can build out from there": You should be able to tell the basics of your story in three to five sentences. If you get that right, filling out the details becomes much easier.

It may also be useful to have a structure for the communications you have with your stakeholders. That can make it clear what the analyst is supposed to do and what the business decision maker or sponsor is supposed to do. For example, at Intuit, George Roumeliotis heads a data science group that analyzes and creates product features based on the vast amount of online data that Intuit collects. For every project in which his group engages with an internal customer, he recommends a methodology for doing and communicating about the analysis. Most of the steps have a strong business orientation:

1. My understanding of the business problem

2. How I will measure the business impact

3. What data is available

4. The initial solution hypothesis

5. The solution

6. The business impact of the solution

Data scientists using this methodology are encouraged to create a wiki so that they can post the results of each step. Clients can review and comment on the content of the wiki. Roumeliotis says that even though there is an online site to review the results, it encourages direct communication between the data scientists and the client.

What Not to Communicate

Since analytical people are comfortable with technical terms—stating the statistical methods used, specifying actual regression coefficients, pointing out the R^2 level (the percentage of variance in the data that's explained by the regression model you are using; see chapter 3) and so forth—they often assume that their audience will be too. But this is a tragic mistake. Most of the audience won't understand a highly technical presentation or report. As one analyst at IHG put it, "Nobody cares about your R^2."

Analysts also are often tempted to describe their analytical results in terms of the sequence of activities they followed to create them: "First we removed the outliers from the data, then we did a logarithmic transformation. That created high autocorrelation, so we created a one-year lag variable . . . " You get the picture. Again, the audiences for analytical results don't really care what process you followed— they only care about results and implications. It may be useful to make such information available in an appendix to a report or presentation, but don't let it get in the way of telling a good story with your data—and start with what your audience really needs to know.

Historical Examples of Communicating Results, Good and Bad

Presentation of quantitative results is a technique that has been used for a long time, and, as now, can successfully convince the intended audience or completely undermine the importance of those results. Let's look at an example of each.

Florence Nightingale: A Good Example of Communicating Results

Florence Nightingale is widely known as the founder of the profession of nursing and a reformer of hospital sanitation methods, but she was also a very early user of quantitative methods. When Nightingale and thirty-eight volunteer nurses were sent in October 1854 to a British military hospital in Turkey during the Crimean

War, she found terrible conditions in a makeshift hospital. Most of the deaths in the hospital were attributable to epidemic, endemic, and contagious disease, and not to the wounds inflicted in battle. In February 1855 the mortality of cases treated in the hospital was 43 percent. Nightingale clearly saw the need for improving basic sanitation at the hospital and believed that statistics could be used to solve the problem. She started to collect data and systematize record-keeping practices, keeping detailed, daily records of admissions, wounds, diseases, treatment, and deaths.

Nightingale's greatest innovation, however, was in presentation of the results. From an early age, Nightingale was interested in numbers and in tabulating information. Although she recognized the importance of proof based on numbers, she also understood that numeric tables were not universally interesting (even when they were much less common than they are today!) and that the average reader would avoid reading them and thereby miss the evidence. As she wanted readers to receive her statistical message, she developed diagrams to dramatize the needless deaths caused by unsanitary conditions, and the need for reform (see figure 4-1). While taken for granted now, it was at that time a relatively novel method of presenting data.

Her innovative diagrams were a kind of pie chart with displays in the shape of wedge cuts. Nightingale printed them in several colors to clearly show how the mortality from each cause changed from month to month. The evidence of the numbers and the diagrams was clear and indisputable.

Nightingale continuously reported to England about the conditions she encountered, always urging reforms. She extensively used the creative diagrams to present reports on the nature and magnitude of the conditions of medical care in the Crimea to members of Parliament who would have been unlikely to read or understand just

FIGURE 4-1

Florence Nightingale's diagram of the causes of mortality in the "Army in the East"

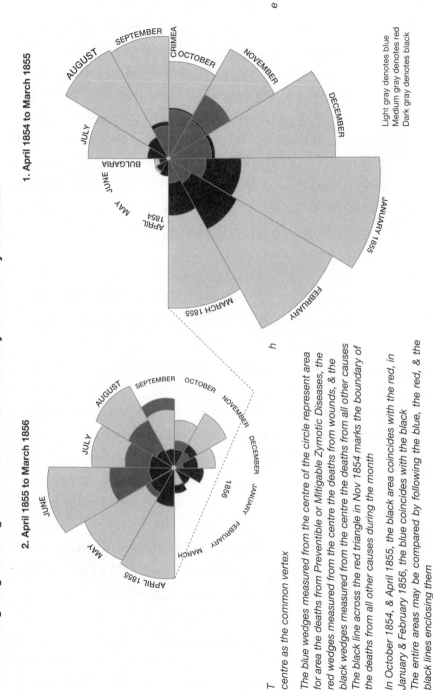

1. April 1854 to March 1855

2. April 1855 to March 1856

Light gray denotes blue
Medium gray denotes red
Dark gray denotes black

The blue wedges measured from the centre of the circle represent area for area the deaths from Preventible or Mitigable Zymotic Diseases, the red wedges measured from the centre the deaths from wounds, & the black wedges measured from the centre the deaths from all other causes The black line across the red triangle in Nov 1854 marks the boundary of the deaths from all other causes during the month

In October 1854, & April 1855, the black area coincides with the red, in January & February 1856, the blue coincides with the black The entire areas may be compared by following the blue, the red, & the black lines enclosing them

103

the numeric tables. People were shocked to find that the wounded soldiers were dying, rather than being cured, in the hospital. Eventually, death rates were sharply reduced, as shown in the data Nightingale systematically collected. The mortality rate continued to fall. When she returned to England in June of 1856 after the Crimean War ended, she found herself a celebrity and praised as a heroine.

Nightingale became a Fellow of the Royal Statistical Society in 1859—the first woman to become a member—and an honorary member of the American Statistical Association in 1874. Karl Pearson, a famous statistician and the founder of the world's first university statistics department, acknowledged Nightingale as a "prophetess" in the development of applied statistics.[4]

Gregor Mendel: A Poor Example of Communicating Results

For a less impressive example of communicating results—and a reminder of how important the topic is—consider the work of Gregor Mendel.[5] Mendel, the father of the concept of genetic inheritance, said a few months before his death in 1884 that, "My scientific studies have afforded me great gratification; and I am convinced that it will not be long before the whole world acknowledges the results of my work." The world did eventually discover Mendel's work, but it took several decades. Perhaps if he had been better at communicating his results, the adoption of his ideas would have happened much more quickly—perhaps while he was still alive.

Mendel, a monk, was the forerunner of the new science of genetics. The leading theory in biology at the time was that inherited traits blended from generation to generation; Mendel's study of the inheritance of certain traits showed rather that the inheritance of genetic information from generation to generation follows particular laws (which were later named after him). The significance of Mendel's work was not recognized until the turn of the twentieth century; the independent rediscovery of these laws formed the foundation of the modern science of genetics.

Mendel hammered out the mathematical principles of inheritance through well-designed and scrupulous experiments in the fields of his monastery. He chose to study in detail the common garden pea, which was cheap, took up little space, and produced offspring quickly (two generations per year). Mendel was able to selectively cross-pollinate purebred plants with specific traits and observe the outcome over many generations.

Between 1856 and 1863 Mendel patiently worked on carefully self-pollinating and wrapping each individual plant to prevent accidental pollination by insects. After eight years of work, Mendel had cultivated 12,980 pea plants from 225 original parent plants from which he drew complex data to detect a pattern or regularity that governs the acquisition of inherited traits. He identified recessive and dominant characteristics, later called genes.

If only Mendel's communication of results had been as effective as his experiments. He published his results in an obscure Moravian scientific journal. It was distributed to more than 130 scientific institutions in Europe and overseas, yet had little impact at the time and was cited only about three times over the next thirty-five years. Mendel's complex and detailed work was not understood even by influential people in the same field. If Mendel had been a professional scientist rather than a monk, he might have been able to project his work more extensively and perhaps publish his work abroad. Mendel did make some attempt to contact scientists overseas by sending Darwin and others reprints of his work; the whereabouts of only a handful are now known. Darwin, it is said, didn't even cut the pages to read Mendel's work.

Although Mendel remarked not long before his death, "My time will come," it is hard to know whether he really believed those words; he died never knowing how profoundly his findings would change history.

Although Mendel's work was both brilliant and unprecedented, it took more than thirty years for the rest of the scientific community to catch up to it—it was not until the early twentieth century that the importance of his ideas was realized, and scientists in the area acknowledged Mendel's priority. The lesson here? If you don't want your outstanding analytical results to be ignored for that long or longer, you must devote considerable attention to the communication of them.

Modern Methods of Communicating Results

These days, there are multiple ways of communicating results that weren't available to Nightingale and Mendel. If you're printing out numbers and simple charts on paper or a screen, you're probably not using all of the tools at your disposal. Of course, the appropriate communications tool depends on the situation and your audience, and you don't want to employ sexy visual analytics simply for the sake of their sexiness.

However, visual analytics (also known as *data visualization*) have advanced dramatically over the last several years. If you're just using bar and pie charts, you're only scratching the surface of what you can do with visual display. "Purposes and Types of Visual Analytics" may not include all of the possible options, but it is one of the more comprehensive lists we have seen.[6] It may seem difficult to decide which kind of chart to use for what purpose, but at some point visual analytics software will do it for you based on the kind of variables in your data. SAS Visual Analytics, for example, is one tool that already does that for its users; the feature is called "Autochart." If the data includes, for example, "One date/time category and any number of other categories or measures," the program will automatically generate a line chart.[7]

Purposes and Types of Visual Analytics

IF YOU WANT TO:

See relationships among data points:

- **Scatterplot:** Shows the relationship between two variables on a two-dimensional grid
- **Matrix plot:** For showing relationships and frequencies for hierarchical variables
- **Heat map:** Individual values contained in a matrix are represented as colors
- **Network diagram:** Shows relationships between entities and the strengths of the paths between them

Compare a set of frequencies or values, typically for one variable:

- **Bar chart:** Length of bar represents values
- **Histogram:** Type of bar chart with bars showing frequencies of data at specified intervals
- **Bubble chart:** Displays a set of numeric values as circles, with the size of the circle corresponding to the value

Show the rise and fall of one variable in relation to another (typically time):

- **Line graph:** Two-dimensional graph, typically with one variable or multiple variables with standardized data values
- **Stack graph:** Line graph with filled-in areas underneath the graph, typically showing change in multiple variables; can also show change in multiple categories with different colors

See the parts of a whole and how they relate to each other:

- **Pie chart:** Displays distribution of values in one variable in a pie format; percentages of each value correspond to size of slices

- **Tree map:** Visual for showing the size of values in a hierarchical variable, such as world/continents/countries/population in each country

Understand data across geography:

- Overlaying summarized data onto geographical maps with colors, bubbles, or spikes representing different values

Analyzing text frequencies:

- **Tag cloud:** A visualization of word frequencies; more frequently used words are displayed in larger type
- **Phrase net:** Shows frequencies of combinations of words used together; more frequently used words are displayed in larger type

The types of visual analytics listed in the worksheet are static, but visual analytics are increasingly becoming dynamic and interactive. Swedish professor Hans Rosling popularized this approach with his frequently viewed TED Talk, which used visual analytics to show the changing population health relationships between developed and developing nations over time.[8] Rosling has created a website called Gapminder (www.gapminder.org) that displays many of these types of interactive visual analytics. It is likely that we will see more of these interactive analytics to show movement in data over time, but they are not appropriate or necessary for all types of data and analyses.

Sometimes you can even get more tangible with your outputs than graphics. For example, Vince Barabba, a market researcher and strategist for several large companies including General Motors, Xerox, and Kodak (their problems weren't his fault!), was a creative thinker when he worked for these firms about how best to communicate market research. At GM, for example, he knew that executives were familiar with assessing the potential of three-dimensional clay models of cars. So at one point, when he had some market research results that were particularly important to get across, he developed a 3-D model of the graphic results that executives could walk through and touch. Seeing and touching a "spike" of market demand was given new meaning by the display.

At IHG, there are several analytics groups, but David Schmitt is head of one in the finance organization called Performance Strategy and Planning. Schmitt's group is supposed to tell "here's what happened," reporting-oriented stories about IHG's performance. They are quite focused on "telling a story with data," and on using all possible tools to get attention for, and stimulate action based on, their results. They have a variety of techniques to do this, depending on the audience. One approach they use is to create "music videos"—five-minute, self-contained videos that get across the broad concepts behind their results using images, audio, and video. They follow up with a verbal presentation that adds supporting information to drive home the meaning behind the concepts.

For example, Schmitt's group recently created a video describing predictions for summer demand. Called "Summer Road Trip," it featured a car going down the road, passing road signs saying "High Demand Ahead" and billboards with market statistics along the side of the road.[9] The goal of the video was to get the audience thinking about what would be the major drivers of performance in the coming period, and how they relate to different parts of the country. As Schmitt notes, "Data isn't the point, numbers aren't the point—it's about the idea." Once the basic idea has been communicated, Schmitt will use more conventional presentation approaches to delve into the data. But he hopes that the minds of the audience members have been primed and conditioned by the video they've just seen.

Games are another approach to communicating analytical results and models. They can be used to communicate how variables interact in complex relationships. For example, the "Beer Game," a simulation based on a beer company's distribution processes, was developed at MIT in the 1960s, and has been used by thousands of companies and students to teach supply chain management models and principles such as the "bullwhip effect"—the oscillation in order volumes resulting from poor information among supply chain participants. Other companies are beginning to develop their own games to communicate specific objectives. Trucking company Schneider National has developed a simulation-based game to communicate the importance of analytical thinking in dispatching trucks and trailers. The goal of the game is to minimize variable costs for a given amount of revenue, and minimize the driver's time at home. Decisions to accept loads or move trucks empty are made by the players, who are aided by decision support tools. Schneider uses the game to help its personnel understand the value of analytical decision aids, to communicate the dynamics of the business, and to change the mind-set of employees from "order takers" to "profit makers." Some Schneider customers have also played the game.

Companies can also use contemporary technology to allow decision makers to interact directly with data. For example, Deloitte Consulting has created an airport operations query and reporting system as an iPad app. It uses Google maps to show on a map the airports to which a particular airline—in this case Delta—flies. Different airplane colors (red for bad, green for good) indicate positive or negative performance at an individual airport. Touching a particular airport's symbol on the map brings up financial and operational data for that particular airport. Touching various buttons can bring up indicators of staffing, customer service levels, finances, operations, and problem areas. This app is only one example of what can be done with today's interactive and user-friendly technologies.

Beyond the Report

Presentations or reports are not the only possible outputs of analytical projects. It's even better if analysts have been engaged to produce an outcome that is closer to creating value. For example, many firms are increasingly embedding analytics into automated decision environments.[10] In insurance, banking, and consumer-oriented pricing environments (such as airlines and hotels), automated decision making based on analytical systems is very common—indeed it is sometimes difficult to get a human to look at your loan or insurance policy application. In these environments, we know analytics will be used because there is no choice in the matter (or at least very little; humans will sometimes review exceptional cases). If you're a quantitative analyst or the owner of an important decision process and you can define your task as developing and implementing one of these systems, it is far more powerful than producing a report.

In the online information industry, companies have big data involving many petabytes of information. New information comes in at such volume and speed that it would be difficult for humans to comprehend it all. In this environment, the data scientists that work in such organizations (basically quantitative analysts with higher-than-normal IT skills) are often located in product development organizations. Their goal is to develop product prototypes and new product features, not reports or presentations.

For example, the Data Science group at the business networking site LinkedIn is a part of the product organization, and has developed a variety of new product features and functions based on the relationships between social networks and jobs. They include People You May Know, Talent Match, Jobs You May Be Interested In, InMaps visual network displays, and Groups You Might Like. Some of these features (particularly People You May Know) have had a dramatic effect on the growth and persistence of the LinkedIn customer base.

If you or the quantitative analysts in your organization are primarily working on internal problems and processes, then the deliverable still doesn't need to be just a report or presentation. The goal is to actually improve the process or decision, so you or your analysts will need to engage in whatever it takes to bring those improvements about. When Tom did some research on how companies improved fifty-seven different decisions a few years ago, he found that analytics was the factor that was most often mentioned as a means to bring about improvement.[11] But "culture and leadership changes" were second, "better data" was third, and "changing the business process" was fourth. On average, the companies interviewed mentioned more than five different factors that were responsible for the improvement in decisions. That means that analysts have to be more than analysts; they have to be consultants in business change.

When Results Don't Imply Actions

We expect that the results from quantitative analysis will lead to action, but sometimes perfectly good results don't translate into specific actions, although they are still useful to know. For example, Jinho once collaborated on a study of the value of moving first in the game Go. Go, one of the oldest strategic board games in the world, takes simple elements (lines and black and white lens-shaped pieces, or "stones") and applies simple rules. Yet despite the apparent simplicity, the game generates subtleties that have enthralled players for thousands of years.[12] In Asia, especially in Korea, Japan, and China, tens of millions of people enjoy playing Go, and nearly a thousand professionals make their living competing in tournaments that offer millions of dollars in prize money.

At the beginning of the game the board is empty. One player takes the black stones and the other player the white stones. Black and

White alternate turns, with Black moving first. That confers an advantage, but no one had ever studied just how much an advantage. Since 1974, in professional games 5.5 points have been given to White at the start of a game to compensate for Black's having the first move. This is called *komi*.

Jinho analyzed data from 577 professional games in Korea to understand whether 5.5 points is the right value of komi. The results suggested that it was too small overall. However, a complication emerged in the analysis. The data suggested that moving first is an advantage only for the player who is skillful enough to use it. One theoretically plausible action that might be taken based on these results is komi discrimination—that is, both (1) maintaining the current level of komi (5.5 points) for those players moving first whose play indicates that the current komi is not likely to be associated with winning a game, and (2) increasing the komi for other players. It seems unlikely that such komi discrimination would be acceptable in professional tournaments. Therefore, a good analysis (that led to a prominent publication for Jinho and his colleague in an academic journal) did not lead to any specific action.[13]

Summary

We've now described each of the three stages and six steps in the model for how to think analytically. If you can put together each of the steps outlined in chapters 2, 3, and 4 in an analysis, you can analyze and solve almost any quantitative problem. Even if you don't have a highly quantitative background, you can perform most of these steps. Actual statistical or mathematical analysis takes place only in a couple of them. And computers can do most of the dirty work for you in such cases.

The key to success is to make sure that the beginning and ending steps of the analysis are well thought out. If the problem is identified and framed correctly, the intermediate steps will usually be relatively straightforward. And if you don't communicate the results effectively, no action will take place—so that's a really important step as well.

Analytical Thinking Example: A Practical Theory for Predicting Divorce

A newlywed couple went to a brilliant mathematician who was famous for predicting whether newlyweds are heading for a lifetime of happiness or spiraling toward divorce. They were asked to sit opposite each other in a room on their own and to talk about a contentious issue for fifteen minutes. Analyzing the recorded conversation of the couple, he predicted: "You guys might as well get divorced right away." It was well known that his predictions were astonishingly accurate. The mathematician who worked on models of whether loving couples are bound to spend their lives together or end their marriages in divorce is James Murray, a professor at Oxford University. He collaborated with John Gottman, a professor and psychologist at the University of Washington, on the research. Gottman supplied the hypotheses and the data—collected in videotaped and coded observations of many couples—and a long-term interest in what makes marriages successful. Murray supplied the expertise on nonlinear models. After the research was done, Gottman was particularly successful at communicating his results to couples around the world. Let's examine their approach within the six-step framework—with an emphasis on communication of results.

PROBLEM RECOGNITION AND FRAMING. The rise in divorce rates in developed countries, including the United States, is a widespread, significant, and poorly understood phenomenon. However, without a theoretical understanding of the processes related to marital stability and dissolution, it is difficult to design and evaluate new marriage interventions. If you can build a mathematical framework for a long-lasting marriage, it will provide the foundation for a scientific theory of marital relations. Murray and Gottman undertook to devise the formula for marital interactions.

REVIEW OF PREVIOUS FINDINGS. Calculating the odds of a happy marriage is nothing new, but divorce predictions have been neither rigorous nor accurate. Murray and Gottman took it a step further than most: they teamed up to create a mathematical model that predicts with astonishing accuracy whether couples will divorce. Gottman had been researching marriage- and divorce-related behaviors for years, so he was familiar with the territory.

MODELING (VARIABLE SELECTION). Murray and Gottman noted that the conversation reflected a couple's underlying problems, and that argument, laughter, teasing, and displays of affection during the conversation created emotional connection. Specifically they focused on the following responses: humor, agreement, joy, affection, interest, anger, domination, sadness, whining, belligerence, defensiveness, disgust, stonewalling, and contempt.

DATA COLLECTION (MEASUREMENT). Researchers invited couples to participate in a laboratory study. Seven hundred newlywed couples participated. They were asked to sit opposite each other in a room by themselves, and then asked to talk about a contentious issue, such as money, sex, or relations with the in-laws. Each couple was told to talk about this topic—one at which they had been at loggerheads for some time—for an entire fifteen minutes while being filmed. Observers then watched the film and awarded the husband and wife positive or negative points depending on what was said. The pairs who showed affection, humor, or happiness while they talked were given the maximum points, while those who displayed contempt or belligerence received the minimum. Contempt was deemed more destructive than disgust, sadness, or anger. The points range from +4 to −4 as follows:

Humor: +4	Sadness: −1
Agreeing: +4	Whining: −1
Joy: +4	Belligerence: −2
Affection: +4	Defensiveness: −2
Interest: +2	Stonewalling: −2
Anger: −1	Disgust: −3
Domineering: −1	Contempt: −4

DATA ANALYSIS. Murray and Gottman's job was to identify the patterns that are predictive of divorce or of a happy marriage. First, the scores were plotted on a graph; the point at which the two lines met illustrated the marriage's chances of success or failure. If either the husband or the wife were consistently negative, then they were assumed to be candidates for divorce. The key turned out to be quantifying the ratio of positive to negative interactions during the talk. The magic ratio is 5:1, and a marriage can be in trouble when it falls below this. The results were put into a mathematical model using difference equations that highlight underlying character traits predicting a marriage's success.

Using the resulting scores, they divided the couples into five groups as follows:

> *Validating couple:* Calm, intimate, like to back each other up and share a companionable relationship. They prefer shared experience to individuality.

Avoiders: Do their best to eschew confrontation and conflict. They respond only positively to each other.

Volatile couple: Are romantic and passionate but have heated arguments. They are a mix of stable and unstable, but generally tend to be more unhappy than not.

Hostile couple: One partner does not want to talk about an issue and the other agrees, so there is no communication.

Hostile-detached couple: One is fiery and wanting to argue, while the other one is just not interested in discussing the issue.

The mathematical model characterized the differences between two types of stable couples (validating couple and avoiders), whose marriages are likely to last, from two types of unstable couples (hostile and hostile-detached couple). The volatile couple group was predicted to stay married—despite having an unstable marriage.

The seven hundred couples who participated in the study were then contacted at one- to two-year intervals over a period of twelve years. Murray and Gottman's formula correctly predicted the divorce rate with an accuracy of 94 percent. The reason the test is only 94 percent accurate is that some volatile couples, whom the researchers thought would stay married and unhappy, actually ended up getting divorced.

RESULTS PRESENTATION AND ACTION. The model was published in a book by Gottman, Murray, and their colleagues called *The Mathematics of Marriage: Dynamic Nonlinear Models.* This book was primarily intended for other academics. But unlike many academics (and unlike Murray), Gottman was also very interested in influencing the actual practices of his research subjects. He has published a variety of books and articles on the research, and has created (with his wife Julie) the Gottman Relationship Institute (www.gottman.com), which provides training sessions, videos on relationship improvement, and a variety of other communications vehicles. This work also holds promise for therapists, giving them new tools for helping couples overcome destructive communication patterns which can send them rushing down the road toward divorce. The Gottman Institute has created a set of instructional materials and workshops for therapists as well. Finally, the model also allows researchers to simulate couples' reactions under various circumstances. Thus, modeling leads to "what if" thought experiments which can be used to help design new scientifically based intervention strategies for troubled marriages.

Gottman helped create the largest randomized clinical trial (a mad scientist story), using more than ten thousand couples in the research. Gottman notes how the research helps actual couples: "For the past eight years I've been really involved, working with my amazingly talented wife, trying to put these ideas together and use our theory so that it helps couples and babies. And we now know that these interventions really make a big difference. We can turn around 75 percent of distressed couples with a two-day workshop and nine sessions of marital therapy."[14]

That's what we call effective communication and action!

Analytical Thinking Example: FICO Score

The FICO score, a three-digit number between 300 and 850, is a snapshot of a person's financial standing at a particular point in time.[15] When you apply for credit—whether for a credit card, a car loan, or a mortgage—lenders want to know what risk they'd take by loaning money to you. FICO scores are the credit scores most lenders use to determine your credit risk. Your FICO scores affect both how much and what loan terms (interest rate, etc.) lenders will offer you at any given time. It is a fantastic example of converting analytics into action, since just about all lenders in the United States—and growing numbers outside of the United States—make use of it. Let's look at how it was developed within the six-step framework.

PROBLEM RECOGNITION AND FRAMING. Credit scores give lenders a fast, objective measurement of a client's credit risk. Before the use of scoring, the credit-granting process could be slow, inconsistent, and unfairly biased. Engineer Bill Fair and mathematician Earl Isaac came up with the idea that better business decisions could be made if they could calculate statistically the risk of default by taking into account various factors in an applicant's personal and financial history. They set up a company in 1956 to develop the model and started to sell their first credit-scoring system two years later. The first general-purpose FICO score debuted in 1989.

REVIEW OF PREVIOUS FINDINGS. Credit reporting was born more than one hundred years ago, when small retail merchants banded together to trade financial information about their customers. The merchant associations then morphed into small credit bureaus, which subsequently consolidated into larger ones with the advent of computerization. However, a general-purpose credit score was not even close to a fledgling stage.

MODELING (VARIABLE SELECTION). Among the different credit data in a credit report, Fair and Isaac selected the following variables, which can be grouped into five categories (variables like age, gender, race, nationality, and marital status were excluded), as shown in table 4-1.

TABLE 4-1

Fair and Isaac's credit analysis variables

Payment history	Account payment information on specific types of accounts; presence of adverse public records, collection items, and/or delinquency; severity of delinquency; amount past due on delinquent accounts or collection items; time since past due items, adverse public records or collection items; number of past due items on file; number of accounts paid as agreed
Amounts owed	Amount owing on accounts; amount owing on specific types of accounts; lack of a specific type of balance, in some cases; number of accounts with balances; proportion of credit lines used; proportion of installment loan amounts still owing
Credit history span	Time since accounts opened; time since accounts opened by specific type of account; time since account activity
New credit	Number of recently opened accounts, and proportion of recently opened accounts by type of account; number of recent credit inquiries; time since recent account opening(s) by type of account; time since credit inquiry(s); reestablishment of positive credit history following past payment problems
Types of credit used	Number of various types of accounts

DATA COLLECTION (MEASUREMENT). Americans' financial habits are monitored by one or more of the three national credit-reporting agencies (CRAs): Equifax, Experian, and Trans Union. Every month, financial institutions or creditors send the CRAs credit files, which include consumers' account numbers, types of credit (e.g., mortgages, credit card loans, automobile loans), outstanding balances, collection actions, and bill-payment histories. Data about an individual consumer can vary from agency to agency. Since the FICO score is based on information the CRA keeps on file about you, you have three FICO scores: one for each of the three CRAs.

DATA ANALYSIS. In general, a credit score takes into account a lot of different information from a consumer's credit report, but it is not all treated equally. Some aspects of your credit history are more important than others and will weigh more heavily on your overall score. The FICO score is calculated from a proprietary formula owned exclusively by Fair and Isaac. Although the exact components of the formula and the method of calculation are not available for publication (and each CRA has its own specific algorithm for calculating the score), FICO has disclosed the following components:

35 percent: Payment history

30 percent: Credit utilization

15 percent: Credit history span

10 percent: Types of credit

10 percent: Recent inquiries

RESULTS PRESENTATION AND ACTION. FICO does not maintain a database of FICO scores. Instead, when a lender requests a credit rating, the score is generated by one of the CRAs from which the lender has requested the report. FICO provides the CRAs with software containing an algorithm—a mathematical formula derived from random samples of consumers' credit information—which is used to calculate the score. However, since each CRA has modified its algorithm slightly, scores differ across CRAs.

The FICO score ranges between 300 and 850. The best credit rates are given to people with scores above 770, but a score of 700 is considered good. The median score is about 725. When the score dips below the mid-600s, those consumers generally qualify only for "subprime" lending and the interest rate starts to climb significantly.

FICO scores, the most-used credit scores in the world, have dramatically improved the efficiency of US credit markets by improving risk assessment. It gives the lender a better picture of whether the loan will be repaid, based entirely upon a consumer's loan history. A growing number of companies having nothing to do with the business of offering credit (such as insurance companies, cellular phone companies, landlords, and affiliates of financial service firms) are now scrutinizing the data on credit reports and using this information to decide whether to do business with a consumer and to determine rate tiers for different grades of consumers. Some employers are even checking credit scores when hiring to possibly determine who would make a good employee. Many automobile insurance companies use it to determine your overall level of financial responsibility, which they view as highly correlated with your driving responsibility. In short, it is one of the greatest successes of the application of analytical thinking in history.

Analytical Thinking Example: Birth of a New Concept in Value Stores

In May 1999, Homeplus entered the hypermarket sector in Korea by forming a joint venture with Tesco. At the time the hypermarket sector in Korea was a "red ocean"—filled with blood as eleven players in strong competition battled it out. Not only local retailers such as E-mart, Lotte Magnet, Kim's Club, Hanaro Mart, LG Mart, Mega Mart, Aram Mart, and Top Mart, but also Western retailers equipped with capital joined the unlimited competition. Homeplus jumped into this difficult sector as the twelfth player, but created "10-10" legendary success, achieving ten trillion Korean-won sales in just in ten years. In these ten years, Homeplus created 47 percent annual average sales growth and 175 percent profit growth, overtaking early starters. The secrets behind Homeplus's big success are the leadership of Homeplus CEO SH Lee, and his strategy of "nothing for it but to win." Lee's strategy was a new weapon developed from thorough market research: the "value store" concept that completely turned around the conventional notion about hypermarket. While the research was not generally statistical, it can still be discussed using the six-step model.

PROBLEM RECOGNITION AND FRAMING. Homeplus was well aware that it could not be successful just by making stores the same as its many competitors. It had to create a totally different store concept that was clearly differentiated from other existing hypermarkets. What could that concept be? Amid a flood of ideas and marketing theories, Homeplus found the answer in the principle that "customers come first." Existing hypermarkets were the "warehouse" type that copied the European or American model. Shop floors were filled with flat and boring racks and shelves with piles of packed boxes displayed. Thorough research and analysis on customer needs was the only way to understand what customers really wanted from hypermarkets.

REVIEW OF PREVIOUS FINDINGS. Existing market research on hypermarket customers was not accessible because it was other retailers' confidential data. CEO Lee's motto was that the way to become the world's best retailer was, "Take the best, and make it better." That meant clearly understanding what the current world's best was doing and exceeding it. In order to learn the latest trends in the global retail market, Homeplus benchmarked various retails channels, such as hypermarkets, supermarkets, category killers, department stores, and multicomplex shopping centers in twenty-five countries, including America, Japan, Europe, and Southeast Asia; the goal was to take the learning and make Homeplus better.

MODELING (VARIABLE SELECTION). The variables included in the retailer and customer research included:

- Shopping venue and the reason for selecting the shopping venue

- Purpose of shopping, satisfaction level, complaints

DATA COLLECTION (MEASUREMENT). Data for the research was gathered through two primary methods:

- Visits and analysis of various retailers around the world

- Comprehensive and structured market research and customer surveys of South Korean customers by an independent research agency

DATA ANALYSIS. The result of extensive data analysis was striking. Price was not the only thing customers needed. It was an important requirement, but what customers really wanted was high value—a reasonable price that took into account their time and use of the products. They also wanted their value as customers to be recognized, so they wanted the premium look and feel of a department store and matching quality of service. What was even more important was that customers wanted not only to buy various products at low prices, but also to enjoy "one-stop-living services" in a pleasant shopping environment. Therefore, the new hypermarket concept Homeplus had to pursue was the "value store," which would not only sell a wide range of products at low prices, but also provide the "living values" that customers truly wanted—kind service, a pleasant shopping environment, convenient facilities, various education programs (a strong cultural value in South Korea), and exciting culture/entertainment services.

RESULTS PRESENTATION AND ACTION. The design of the first Homeplus store in Ansan included a shopping environment as pleasant as a department store, and convenient facilities providing one-stop-living services on the ground floor, including a food court with four hundred seats, a pharmacy, a clinic, an optical shop, a laundromat, a bank, a kids' playground, a nursing room, and even a government

Public Service Center issuing identification cards. A Culture Center made the store not only a shopping venue, but the biggest community center in the store's service area. All the retail experts who looked around the Homeplus shop floor before its opening shook their heads, saying the fundamentals of hypermarket design were ignored. It made no sense to them to put relatively unprofitable convenience facilities in the expensive space on the ground floor. The hypermarket business was described as a "space game," and space equaled money, so the rule was to maximize sales within the given space. No wonder putting a Culture Center on the first floor was viewed as "nonsense." Visitors from Tesco, Homeplus's joint venture partner, also questioned the arrangement: "Isn't it better to show customers fresh food when they enter the ground floor? Isn't that the layout best suited to the nature of retailing?" SH Lee answered, "The CEO made the decision. Customers are the CEO," and pushed ahead with the plan.

The Homeplus Ansan store, the first value store in Korea, hit record-high sales on its opening day. Sales were 1.5 times that of two nearby competitors' stores combined, and the 100,000 customers on opening day almost equaled the number of residents within a 5 km radius. Customers were surprised at the look and feel of the store and facilities that were clearly different from anything they had seen. Despite this, retail experts predicted that Homeplus would not be able to last for more than a year. However, Homeplus kept breaking records every time it opened a new store, and continued to grow quickly. The Yongdeongpo store in Seoul, which opened in 2001, recorded sales that exceeded even a department store. The explosive growth enhanced the store's reputation not only locally but internationally. Some investment analysts noted:

> "Homeplus created an artistic harmony of wet market feel and advanced retailing techniques."

"The store concept was outstanding compared to competitors"

"Homeplus sales were unbelievable"

Other competitors began to convert their warehouse stores to value stores, but Homeplus continued to offer distinctive services, including schools for adult education. Homeplus operates Homeplus Schools in 110 out of 124 stores nationwide as of 2011, with over one million members a year and six thousand instructors. This is the biggest adult learning operation in the world. The greatest benefit of Homeplus School is its impact on customer loyalty. Many customers cite Homeplus School as the first reason why they like Homeplus. An average Homeplus School member spends twice as much per visit as a normal customer, and visits twice as frequently. The word-of-mouth buzz spread by one million Homeplus School members is a powerful engine to enhance Homeplus brand value.

5

Quantitative Analysis and Creativity

Around 275 BC, a young man went to a public bath. When he stepped into a tub of water, the water began to spill over the sides. He suddenly leaped out of the bath and rushed home naked, crying, "Eureka, eureka!" People who saw him thought he was mad. This young man was Archimedes, and *eureka* in Greek means "I have found it." We'll describe shortly what he found and why he was so excited about finding it. Let's just say now, however, that he used both creativity and quantitative analysis in the solution to his problem.

It's often felt that creativity is the opposite of quantitative analysis. Creativity is viewed as being exploratory, free thinking, inspiration based, and visionary. Quantitative analysis is often viewed as being tedious, rote, and by the numbers. We feel strongly, however, that creativity and analytics are hardly opposites, and are often closely related. The most successful uses of analytics are highly creative (as we hope you have seen in the examples we've already provided), and creativity is an important component of successful analytical approaches to problems. We'd also argue that creativity alone—without any data or analytics—usually does not provide enough support for making the best decisions. We've always found that the most successful people and organizations use both creativity and analytics.

For example, Apple is often described as one of the most creative companies on the planet today. Indeed, the company's products are developed in a highly creative fashion. However, the same creative company employs rigorous processes and analytics in its supply chain operations to ensure that it has the right products at the right time for sale. In its Apple retail stores, for example, it collects and analyzes considerable amounts of data. One article reported, "Once a product goes on sale, the company can track demand by the store and by the hour, and adjust production forecasts daily."[1] An open job description for a supply chain management position at Apple requires, among other things, that the successful applicant "Must combine a working knowledge of world-class supply chain practices, strong analytical capabilities, and business savvy."[2] If even highly creative companies like Apple require analytical orientations in many of their employees, we'll probably see many more combinations of creativity and analytics in the future.

Of course, creativity combined with analytics can be dangerous. You may be aware of Darrell Huff's famous 1954 book, *How to Lie with Statistics*; the title correctly suggests that the analytically devious can use quantitative approaches to at least stretch the truth.[3] We've often heard others say (usually kiddingly) that, "We tortured the statistics until they confessed." There is a thin line between appropriate and inappropriate creativity in the use of analytics. The key discriminating factor is whether or not you are sincerely pursuing the truth. If you're using creativity with analytics in the service of proving your own (or your boss's) idea correct—and if the numbers are making that extremely difficult—it's better to stop being creative and move on to a different hypothesis.

A Quick Review of the Six Steps

It's worth a quick review on how creativity fits into the six-step analytical thinking process that we've described in chapters 2, 3, and 4. Then we'll describe a creative process that can overlay it.

In the *problem recognition and framing* step, creativity is extremely useful and important. Half the battle in problem solving and decision making is framing the problem or decision in a creative way so that it can be addressed effectively. This is the place in the analytical thinking process where the analyst creates a hypothesis for what is going on in the data—often a very creative and intuitive act. Given a particular organizational or business context and a set of constraints, creative framing can change the context, view it in different ways, and reduce or eliminate constraints. For example, in the wine-value equation described in chapter 3, Orley Ashenfelter framed the problem of the value of wine as something that could be predicted using only weather-related variables and the age of wine. Similarly, in the marriage study described in chapter 4, James Murray and John Gottman had the creative insight that continued success in a marital relationship could be predicted by a set of behaviors between the spouses. Often, the creativity used in analytical decisions is the recognition that seemingly complex factors can be predicted or explained by relatively simple and measurable ones.

Admittedly, the *review of previous findings* is probably not the most creative step, but there is creativity in identifying what previous findings or analytical techniques might be relevant to the existing problem. For example, the technique of "survival analysis" was traditionally applied to understand the rate and circumstances under which people or other living organisms died. One researcher, however—Junxiang Lu—has successfully applied it to predicting customer lifetime value in the telecommunications industry.[4] Other researchers have applied it to other marketing-related problems such as determining when a customer is in the market for a product.[5]

The *modeling (variable selection)* step, despite its analytical-sounding name, can also be very creative—particularly for those who are the first to employ a particular model. The choice of variables in a model will sometimes be obvious, depending on intuition or previous findings, but it can sometimes be a creative act. Recall, for example, the use of word length as a predictor of authorship of the Mark Twain letters, described in chapter 3. That was a moderately creative choice for Claude Brinegar, who read about it in the literature, but an extremely clever approach by Thomas Mendenhall, who was apparently the first to use it in his studies of Shakespeare authorship. Of course, if you use the same modeling approach and variables as everyone else to solve the same kind of problem, you are likely to come up with the same results—so why bother doing it at all?

Data collection itself can be a tedious process, but deciding what data to collect can be very creative. Whether you want to study the behaviors of humans, rats, or atoms, there is probably some way to measure and observe the phenomena you care about that no one has thought of.

For example, the social psychologists Mihaly Csikszentmihalyi and Reed Larson wanted to research teenagers' attitudes and feelings. In order to collect data on how the teenagers were feeling throughout the day, the project relied on a unique research method. The researchers gave beepers (paging devices) to seventy-five high school students and had teams of graduate students page them at random points during the day to discover their self-reported feelings at that moment. The data collection method, called the *experience sampling method,* is now widely used.[6]

While the researchers weren't surprised to find that the teens were unhappy most of the time, they were surprised to learn that their emotions turned positive when they were absorbed in performing challenging tasks. The resulting 1984 book, *Being Adolescent: Conflict and Growth in the Teenage Years,* was the first published account of a creative and engaged mental state Csikszentmihalyi labeled *flow,* which became the focus of much of his later work.[7] In effect, he was creatively collecting data on creativity!

The *data analysis* step is not generally one in which creativity is appropriate unless you are really good at math and statistics, and even then you should be conservative. This is the primary point in the analytical thinking process at which creativity can get you into trouble. Every statistical test or mathematical analysis has constraints and assumptions behind it, and you don't want to relax them unless you really know what you are doing.

The *results presentation and action* step, on the other hand, is one in which creativity is vitally important but not often found. Since nonanalytical people won't typically understand analytical results that are presented in technical or mathematical terms, a good analyst needs to think creatively about how the results should be presented in comprehensible—even fun—terms. Don't, for example, talk about the values of coefficients and percentage of variance explained. Instead, use language like, "If we increase spending on advertising by a dollar, on average we get $1.29 in added revenues." That may not sound hugely creative, but it's much more conducive to understanding and action than talking in technical terms, and it requires some creativity to think of such translations.

The Four Stages of Creative Analytical Thinking

We don't want to give you too many stages and steps, but it may be useful to discuss how creative analytical thinking maps onto the six steps we've discussed. In general, the creative process follows these four sequential stages:

Preparation: Doing the groundwork on the problem

Immersion: Intense engagement in solving the problem and the data at hand; a long struggle to find a solution takes place

Incubation: Internalization of the problem into the subconscious mind, with unusual connections likely to be made below the level of consciousness (often just at the time you are frustrated and ready to give up!)

Insight: The big breakthrough in understanding how the problem can be solved through quantitative analysis

Most commonly, the *review of previous findings* stage and a part of the *variable selection stage* fall within the *preparation* section in the process of creative analytical thinking. The *immersion* section corresponds to a part of the *modeling,* all of *data collection,* and a part of the *data analysis* stages. The *incubation* process occurs when *data analysis* comes to an impasse. Then when *insight* suddenly bursts forth, the pieces of the puzzle all fall together. A graphical representation of all of this is in figure 5-1.

Analytical Thinking Example:
Archimedes and the Crown

Let's apply the four stages of the creative process to the six analytical thinking steps in the story of Archimedes—one of the earliest known examples of creative analytical thinking.[8]

FIGURE 5-1

Qualitative analysis and creativity

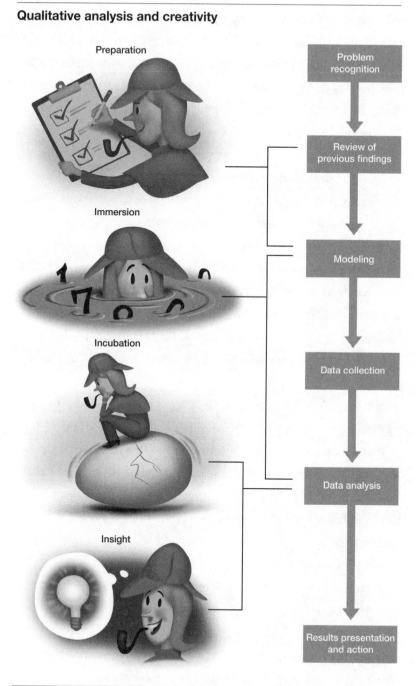

PROBLEM RECOGNITION AND FRAMING. Hieron, the king of Syracuse (in Sicily), vowed to place a golden crown in the shape of a laurel
wreath in the temple of the immortal gods. He weighed out a precise
amount of gold and gave it to a goldsmith for this purpose. On the appointed day the goldsmith delivered to the king's satisfaction an ex-
quisitely wrought crown, which weighed exactly the same as the gold
the king had given to him. However, when the king was preparing for
the ceremony to place the crown in the chosen temple, he heard a
rumor that the crown was not pure gold; that the goldsmith had replaced some of the gold with an equal weight of silver (it was then, as
now, common for goldsmiths to dilute gold with cheaper metals).
Hieron suspected he had been cheated. Not knowing how to detect
the theft, the king posed the question to his advisers, who were unable
to solve the mystery. Finally the king asked Archimedes to solve the
dilemma, *without damaging the crown,* before the day fixed for
the ceremony. Archimedes, twenty-two years old and already famous
for his work in mathematics and physics, accepted the challenge.

REVIEW OF PREVIOUS FINDINGS. There was no specific approach to
measure the volume of any irregularly shaped object; Archimedes himself had to find the method to perform this. This is where he jumped
into the *preparation* creative stage. Archimedes, perhaps one of the
greatest mathematicians and inventors of all time, could measure the
volume of most of regular objects. He reasoned that, because gold weighs
more than silver, a crown mixed with silver would have to be bulkier
(i.e., have greater volume) to weigh the same as one made only of gold.
The problem was how the volume of irregularly shaped objects like the
crown could be measured with precision and without damaging them.

MODELING (VARIABLE SELECTION). Still in *preparation* mode,
Archimedes knew that the volume of the crown would be the key

variable to predict the purity of the crown. Actually measuring the volume successfully, however, required deep *immersion* in the problem and the data. The simplest way of measuring the volume of the crown was to melt it down, mold it into a cube, and measure its dimensions. He couldn't do that because he had been ordered not to damage the crown. He became obsessed with solving the problem and pondered it for quite a while. However, even after a long struggle, the problem remained intractable.

DATA COLLECTION. Immersed in the problem, Archimedes could begin to collect some data. He found out the densities of gold and silver, and hypothesized that a mix of the two might contain as much as 30 percent silver. Still, however, the volume of the wreath-shaped crown would need to be measured, and he didn't know how to do it.

DATA ANALYSIS. The day of the ceremony was drawing nearer. Frustrated, Archimedes almost gave up, even though his reputation as a genius mathematician and physicist would be severely harmed. However, because of the depth of his commitment to the problem, it had become internalized into his subconsciousness: he was in *incubation* mode. One day, to comfort his fatigued spirit and body, Archimedes went to a public bath. When he stepped into a tub of water (a different form of immersion!), the water began to spill over the sides. He suddenly realized that the volume of water displaced must be equal to the volume of the part of his body that was submerged. This meant that the volume of irregular objects could be measured with precision: if he placed the crown into a given amount of water and it displaced more water than the same weight of pure gold, then the crown and the pure gold must have different volume measurements. He leaped out of the bath and ran naked through the streets of Syracuse, shouting out for joy, "Eureka, eureka!" Clearly

Archimedes had finally achieved an *insight*. He ran the test, submerging the crown and then the lump of gold, and the results of the displacement of each of the articles were different. He concluded that the crown was not pure gold, and that the goldsmith had indeed mixed another metal into the gold to cheat the king.

RESULTS PRESENTATION AND ACTION. Archimedes reported his findings to King Hieron, who was delighted by the brilliance of Archimedes' insight. Through this, Archimedes' reputation as a genius mathematician and physicist was heightened greatly. It didn't work out well for everyone, however; the dishonest goldsmith was executed.

Creativity could be defined as *the ability to develop original and useful ideas*. But the Archimedes example suggests that from a quantitative analysis perspective, creativity is just the *facility to grasp a new relationship among the variables* after having identified and selected relevant variables and measuring them. According to this definition, you can learn, teach, exercise, and practice creativity. People can improve their creativity through the acquisition of analytical skills. Companies can achieve the same capacity by running an analytics education program for employees and building an organizational culture that encourages analytical thinking at work.

Immersion and Hard Work as the Source of Creativity and Insight

Thomas Edison famously said, "Genius is ninety-nine percent perspiration and one percent inspiration." Creativity is an insight that suddenly ignites at an unexpected moment to solve a problem. Then where does creativity come from? We believe that creativity comes through earnest effort. Creative analytical thinking and the insight to which it leads are not innate, random characteristics; they are the reward for the ninety-nine percent perspiration—the labor exerted in the process of quantitative analysis: searching previous findings, selecting then measuring relevant variables, then striving to find a pattern underlying the variables. When you immerse yourself in strenuous endeavor, without surrender, you will one day, at an unforeseen moment, run into a *eureka* insight. That's exactly what happened to Archimedes, Newton, and many other geniuses.

Barbara McClintock, an American scientist, was named a 1983 Nobel Laureate for her discovery of genetic transposition. She is the only woman to receive an unshared Nobel Prize in Physiology or Medicine. During her long field research, she frequently experienced these *eureka* moments. She stated definitively that her source of inspiration was being absorbed in her work, completely identifying with the work, and even forgetting herself:

> McClintock got to know every one of her corn plants so intimately that when she studied their chromosomes, she could truly identify *with* them: "I found that the more I worked with them the bigger and bigger [they] got, and when I was really working with them I wasn't outside, I was down there. I was part of the system. I even was able to see the internal parts of the chromosomes—actually everything was there. It surprised me because I actually felt as if I were right down there and these were my friends . . . As you look at these things, they become part of you. And you forgot yourself. The main thing about it is you forgot yourself."[9]

Of course, creativity and hard work are not only associated in the quantitative realm. They also apply to art and literature, for example. Cho Jung Rae, a famous Korean author, also asserts that inspiration does not spark suddenly, but gushes from a very long accumulation of painstakingly hard work and immersion:

> You keep focusing on and immersing in one thing; keep piling up various ideas, and then, at a certain moment in a flash, inspiration strikes you and you understand instantly what you have been desperately looking for. People say inspiration occurs suddenly. Yes, that is true if you only look at the exact moment of inspiration. However, in the process there must be painstakingly hard work and immersion over an extended period of time. Consequently you can put it like this: The depth of painstakingly hard work, and the strength of the immersion determine the inspiration.[10]

In general, intuition is viewed as thoughts that come to mind quickly and without apparent reflection. This insinuates that intuition leads to direct perception of truth without any necessary justification or reasoning process. However, we believe that intuition is an ability that one can acquire primarily through the continuous repetition of analysis, quantitative and otherwise. Neurobiology suggests that neurons can be "trained" through continuous analysis, and thus we believe that intuition is naturally developed when one can figure out, based on experience accumulated over time, an underlying pattern among variables without collecting and analyzing data. Georg Hegel, the German philosopher, felt that only the person who thinks highly analytically can have pure and true intuition.[11]

The Role of Pattern Finding in Analytical Creativity

The essence of creative data analysis is in finding a pattern among the variables in the data. This pattern denotes a regular relationship hidden in the variables. At this stage, mathematical thinking is very helpful, because mathematics itself is the science of patterns: Euclidean geometry, the first great science in ancient Greece, originated from extracted geometrical patterns in nature; Pythagoras's theorem is the pattern in the three sides of a right triangle.

Pattern finding in contemporary organizations tends to come more through statistical analysis than pure math. Certain statistical tools are excellent at showing that a pattern exists in data at a rate greater than would be expected by chance. An analysis might suggest, for example, that customers with a certain purchase pattern (or lack thereof) are likely to stop buying altogether. Or that customers who buy a particular book are likely to buy another one—for example, Amazon's well-known recommendation feature. (A friend of Tom's actually received a recommendation from Amazon saying that people who bought one of Tom's books also were likely to buy a joke gift of simulated dog excrement!). See table 5-1 for a description of different pattern types and the open-source and commercial software that finds them.

Analytical Thinking Example: Beer and Diapers

For a more detailed example of pattern finding, take the most commonly mentioned finding in data mining—that men who drop by a grocery store as the weekend approaches buy both diapers and beer. The finding took place not in ancient Greece, but in Chicago in 1992. It is definitely an example of pattern finding, but it's not a good example of analytical thinking overall (however, we think negative examples can be instructive too).[12]

PROBLEM RECOGNITION AND FRAMING. Thom Blischok, then manager of a retail consulting group at the data warehouse firm Teradata, and his staff were doing an analysis of retail point-of-sale

TABLE 5-1

Data-mining software for finding patterns in data

Tasks	Description	Open-source			Commercial (all multipurpose)
		Single-purpose	Multipurpose		
Regression	Finding a function that fits the data				Microsoft Analysis Services
Classification	Sorts data into one of several predefined classes	CART ML-Flex	RapidMiner R KNIME Weka Orange		SAS: Enterprise Miner Oracle Data Mining IBM-SPSS Modeler STATISTICA KNIME LIONsolver Datameer Analytics Solution
Clustering	Finds groups of objects (clusters)	Carrot2 ELKI			
Sequential association analysis	Searches for relationships between variables	JHepWork ARtool			
Anomaly detection	Identifies unusual data records	ELKI JHepWork			
Text mining	Derives patterns and trends from text	GATE NLTK UIMA RapidMiner			

(POS) data for their client, Osco Drug. As one team member, John Earle, put it, the objective was "looking for affinities between what items were purchased on a single ticket. Then we suggested tests for moving merchandise in the store to see how it affected affinities."[13] Earle goes on to suggest that a primary goal of the analysis was to demonstrate the value of the technology, rather than to solve any particular problem or address a particular decision within Osco.

REVIEW OF PREVIOUS FINDINGS. There was not much in the way of previous findings, except that the team knew that baby-related items were highly profitable, so there was a goal of finding items that might drive or increase their sales.

MODELING (VARIABLE SELECTION). Purchase frequencies of various items in drugstore POS data.

DATA COLLECTION. Osco had the data from its POS systems and made it available to the Teradata team for analysis. The database being analyzed contained purchase data for 1.2 million market baskets (all the items bought in a particular shopping transaction) from about twenty-five Osco Drug stores.

DATA ANALYSIS. There are much more sophisticated data-mining approaches available today, but in 1992 these were not widely used at all. The Teradata team simply formulated database queries to identify items bought in combination above their normal levels. A component of the analysis by a woman named K. Heath found that customers (they were not actually identified as men) shopping between 5:00 p.m. and 7:00 p.m. on Thursdays and Saturdays did buy beer and diapers to a high degree. No statistical tests were done to ensure that the observed level of affinities could not occur by chance.

RESULTS PRESENTATION AND ACTION. This is where the analysis falls short. It is often stated in apocryphal accounts of the story that the beer and diapers were placed near each other in the stores, or that they were strategically placed far away from each other so that customers would have to traverse the entire store. In fact, none of these things happened. The findings were regarded as an amusing curiosity, and no attempt was made by either the Teradata analysts or Osco management to act on them, or to understand the potential value of acting on them.

We don't know enough to understand why this creative pattern-finding effort was not followed up, but it illustrates the fact that every aspect of the analytical thinking process must be effective if any change is to result. Computers may be able to find patterns in data, but it is humans who make sense of—and act on—those patterns (see "Computers and Patterns: The Case of Pi" and "Patterns in the Leading Digit—A Way to Detect Fraud").

Computers and Patterns: The Case of Pi

Pi (π) is the ratio of the circumference of a circle to its diameter. Pi is approximately equal to 3.141592 in the usual decimal notation. Many formulas from mathematics, science, and engineering involve pi, which makes it the most important mathematical concept outside the Pythagorean theorem.[a]

Pi is an irrational number, which means that its value cannot be expressed exactly as a fraction, and consequently its decimal representation never ends or repeats. That doesn't mean, however, that people—from ancient Babylonians to today's mathematicians—have stopped trying to find a pattern in the many decimal places to which pi has been calculated.

Of course, the advent of digital computers in the twentieth century led to an increased rate of new pi calculation records and generally replaced humans at that task. The current record for the decimal expansion of π stands at five trillion digits. New digits are more a function of advances in computing than human math capability. Still, however, no repeating pattern of digits has been found.

While neither humans nor computers have found a repeat pattern in pi, human mathematicians have found many patterns in the application of pi—which is the new role for human creativity in analytical thinking. For example, in a story told by mathematician David Acheson:

Imagine the surprise, then, in the mid-seventeenth century, when mathematicians found π cropping up in all sorts of places that had, apparently, nothing to do with circles at all. One of the most famous results of this kind is an extra-ordinary connection between π and the odd numbers:

$$\frac{\pi}{4} = 1 - \frac{1}{3} + \frac{1}{5} - \frac{1}{7} + \ldots$$

. . . Surprising *connections* of this kind are just the sort of thing that get mathematicians really excited.[b]

Another connection between pi and even numbers has been found. Moreover, pi shows up in the "famous five" equation developed by the eighteenth-century Swiss mathematician Leonhard Euler, which was voted the "most beautiful mathematical formula ever" in a 1988 poll of mathematicians.

The lesson from pi studies is that even when computers have taken over an important mathematical function, human creativity still finds a way to exert itself. In the application of quantitative analysis to business and organizational life, computers have taken over the great majority of statistical calculations. It is the application of those calculations to decision making where creativity still resides.

a. See "Pi," *Wikipedia,* http://en.wikipedia.org/wiki/Pi; "Ask Dr. Math FAQ: About Pi," *Math Forum,* http://mathforum.org/dr.math/faq/faq.pi.html; "Facts About Pi," *Math Forum,* http://mathforum.org/library/drmath/view/57543.html; *Finding pi:* http://mathforum.org/library/drmath/view/55815.html; *Pre-computer History of pi:* http://personal.bgsu.edu/~carother/pi/Pi2.html.

b. David Acheson, *1089 and All That: A Journey into Mathematics* (Oxford: Oxford University Press, 2002), 14.

The Last Words on Analytics and Creativity

We hope we have demonstrated that analytical thinking and creativity can not only coexist, but that they are highly related. You won't be either a good quantitative analyst, or a good consumer of quantitative thinking, if you don't employ all your creative faculties. Remember, however, that there is a limit to how creative you should be in manipulating and explaining data-based results. Creativity is important, but truth is even more so.

Analytical Thinking Example: Linguistic Ability and Alzheimer's Disease

Alzheimer's disease, or simply Alzheimer's, is a brain dysfunction that causes problems with memory, thinking and behavior. Symptoms usually develop slowly, get worse over time, become severe enough to interfere with daily tasks, then finally cause the patient to

Patterns in the Leading Digit—a Way to Detect Fraud

Ted Hill, a math professor at the Georgia Institute of Technology, gives his students a homework exercise at the beginning of a course: either flip a coin two hundred times and record the actual results, or merely pretend to flip a coin and fake two hundred results. At the next class, he runs his eye over the homework data and easily identifies, to the students' amazement, nearly all those who faked their flips. How can he do that? He knows, through a quite involved calculation, that at some point in a series of two hundred coin-flips, either heads or tails will come up six or more times in a row. Most fakers don't know this and avoid faking long runs of heads or tails, which they erroneously believe to be improbable. At just a glance, Hill can see whether or not there is a run of six heads or tails in a student's two hundred coin-toss results; if there isn't, the student must have faked the flips. There is more to this than a classroom trick: if some kind of expected patterns are not present in data, fakes or frauds must have been involved.

As we all well know that our number system uses the digits 1 through 9, we can easily assume that the odds of randomly obtaining any one of them as the leading digit in a number are 1/9. But, counterintuitively enough, this is not true. The *first-digit law,* also called Benford's Law, states that in lists of numbers from many real-life sources of data, the leading digit is distributed in a specific, nonuniform way: the first digit is 1 about 30 percent of the time, and as the leading digit becomes larger, the frequency gets lower.[a] According to Benford's Law, the precise proportion for a first digit is as follows:

First digit	1	2	3	4	5	6	7	8	9
Odds of obtaining as first digit (%)	30.1	17.6	12.5	9.7	7.9	6.7	5.8	5.1	4.6

This somewhat surprising fact was discovered in 1881 by the American astronomer Simon Newcomb, who noticed that in logarithm tables, the earlier pages were much more worn than the other pages. In 1938 physicist Frank Benford made the same discovery in a much larger amount of data than Newcomb. He analyzed about 20,229 different sets of data, including the areas of rivers, baseball statistics, numbers in magazine articles, and the street addresses of the first 342 people listed in *American Men of Science*. All these seemingly unrelated sets of numbers showed the same first-digit frequency proportion as the worn pages of logarithm tables suggested. This pattern of the leading digit was eventually named Benford's Law in his honor. It is acknowledged that Benford's Law unquestionably applies to many situations in the real world.

Many statisticians and accountants firmly believe that Benford's Law is a relatively simple but powerful tool for identifying potential frauds, embezzlers, tax evaders, and sloppy accountants. The idea behind the concept is simple: if someone makes up a data set, it probably won't follow the distribution Benford's Law predicts. By just looking at the first digit of each data entry and comparing the actual frequency of occurrence with the predicted frequency, one can easily finger concocted data. In general, faked or fraudulent data appear to have far fewer numbers starting with 1, and many more starting with 6, than do true data.

In 1972, the Berkeley economist Hal Varian showed that the law could be used to detect possible fraud in lists of socioeconomic data submitted in support of public planning decisions. Forensic accountant Mark Nigrini gained recognition by applying a system he devised based on Benford's Law to some fraud cases in Brooklyn. Today many income tax agencies are using detection software based on Benford's Law, as are a score of large companies and accounting firms. In America, evidence based on Benford's law is legally admissible in criminal cases at the federal, state, and local levels.

a. "Benford's Law," *Wikipedia,* http://en.wikipedia.org/wiki/Benford%27s_law; Malcolm W. Browne, "Following Benford's Law, or Looking Out for No. 1," *New York Times,* August 4, 1998, http://www.nytimes.com/1998/08/04/science/following-benford-s-law-or-looking-out-for-no-1.html?pagewanted=all&src=pm; "Benford's Law," *Wolfram MathWorld* http://mathworld.wolfram.com/BenfordsLaw.html; T. P. Hill, "The First-Digit Phenomenon," *American Scientist,* July–August 1998; Mark J. Nigrini, "Benford's Law," http://www.nigrini.com/benfordslaw.htm.

die for unknown reasons. Alzheimer's disease accounts for 60 to 80 percent of dementia cases. Approximately 5.3 million Americans and one out of eight people age sixty-five and older (13 percent) have Alzheimer's. Alzheimer's is the sixth-leading cause of death in the United States. Aside from the patient's distress, family members and caregivers of a person with Alzheimer's suffer both emotionally and physically, since the demands of day-to-day care, changing family roles, and difficult decisions about placement in a care facility can be hard to handle.

The cause and progression of Alzheimer's are not well understood. Many researchers have tried to find the association of certain characteristics, or *markers,* of people with a higher risk of Alzheimer's. For example, individuals with low education may be more likely to develop dementia and other diseases because of lifestyle differences associated with education, nutrition, alcohol consumption, and occupational exposures. David Snowdon, a professor at Sanders-Brown Center on Aging at the University of Kentucky, and his colleagues thought that linguistic ability in early life may be a better marker than lifestyle.[14] They speculated that a high level of linguistic ability in early life may act as a buffer to cognitive decline by facilitating mnemonic processes for encoding, organizing, and retrieving information. They conducted a landmark and highly creative study linking the cognitive ability of youth with Alzheimer's disease risk later in life. The choice of a sample population—an order of nuns— and the use of nuns' autobiographies as a source of data were both very creative approaches to analytical thinking. We will now examine their work within the six-step framework.

PROBLEM RECOGNITION AND FRAMING. Determine whether linguistic ability in early life is associated with cognitive functioning and a low risk of Alzheimer's disease in later life.

REVIEW OF PREVIOUS FINDINGS. Many of the procedures employed by Snowdon's team were based on previous work by Dr. David Wekstein and Dr. William Markesbery. In 1989 they began a study of age-associated changes in cognition and functioning in a group of older adults who had agreed to donate their brains upon death. The study's focus was to understand how changes in the brain could be linked to Alzheimer's and other neurological disorders in advanced age.

MODELING (VARIABLE SELECTION). Participants in Snowdon's study were members of the School Sisters of Notre Dame religious congregation in Milwaukee, Wisconsin. From 1991 to 1993, women from the convent who were born before 1917 were asked to join the Nun Study, a longitudinal study of aging and Alzheimer's disease. Of the 1,027 eligible sisters, 678 (66 percent) agreed to participate and gave informed written consent. The participation rate in the Nun Study is relatively high, given that all participants agreed to donate their brains upon death, as well as undergo annual assessments of cognitive and physical function. Snowdon and his team further investigated a subset of ninety-three participants in the Nun Study, who had handwritten autobiographies from early life on file in the convent archives. The variables selected are as follow:

- Linguistic ability in early life (idea density and grammatical complexity)

- Cognitive function (seven different dimensions) and Alzheimer's disease in late life

DATA COLLECTION (MEASUREMENT). These sisters' autobiographies were used to characterize the level of linguistic ability in early life. After an average of four years of training in the convent, each sister wrote an autobiography a few weeks before taking her religious vows. Archival information from the convent indicated that each sister was asked to "... write a short sketch of her own life. This account should not contain more than two to three hundred words and should be written on a single sheet of paper ... include the place of birth, parentage, interesting and edifying events of one's childhood, schools attended, influences that led to the convent, religious life, and its outstanding events."

Two indicators of linguistic ability were derived from each autobiography: idea density and grammatical complexity. *Idea density* was defined as the average number of ideas expressed per ten words. Ideas corresponded to elementary propositions, typically a verb, adjective, adverb, or prepositional phrase. Complex propositions that stated or inferred causal, temporal, or other relationships between ideas also were counted. *Grammatical complexity* was computed using the Developmental Level metric, which classifies sentences according to eight levels of grammatical complexity, ranging from

0 (simple one-clause sentences) to 7 (complex sentences with multiple forms of embedding and subordination).

Cognitive function was assessed by a battery of seven neuropsychological tests. These tests assessed memory, concentration, language, visual-spatial ability, and orientation to time and place. The ninety-three sisters in this study wrote their autobiographies at an average age of twenty-two and had their cognitive function assessed an average of fifty-eight years later, when they were between seventy-five and eighty-seven years old.

DATA ANALYSIS. Low idea density and low grammatical complexity in autobiographies written in early life were associated with low cognitive test scores in late life. Low idea density in early life had stronger and more consistent associations with poor cognitive function than did low grammatical complexity. Among the fourteen sisters who died, neuropathologically confirmed Alzheimer's disease was present in all of those with low idea density in early life and in none of those with high idea density.

RESULTS PRESENTATION AND ACTION. Snowdon and his colleagues concluded that written linguistic performance, the study's measure of cognitive ability in early life, " . . . is a potent marker for cognitive problems, Alzheimer's disease, and brain lesions in late life." This indicates that low linguistic ability in early life could be a subtle symptom of very early changes in the brain that ultimately lead to Alzheimer's disease. These types of studies will allow us to better predict who is at risk for a variety of age-related diseases. They published their study, "Linguistic Ability in Early Life and Cognitive Function and Alzheimer's Disease in Late Life," in the prominent *Journal of the American Medical Association*.[15] Snowdon also wrote a popular book about the nuns called *Aging with Grace: What the Nun*

Study Teaches Us About Leading Longer, Healthier, and More Mean-ingful Lives. According to a review of the book by *Library Journal*:

> Snowdon writes with empathy and affection of these sisters,
> who also generously agreed to donate their brains for post-
> mortem pathological studies. From this research, Snowdon
> explains, it emerged that pathological changes did not always
> correlate with observable changes, that linguistic ability
> seems to protect against Alzheimer's, that prevention of
> stroke and heart diseases can help avoid dementia, and that
> heredity, diet, and exercise also play a part. Blending personal
> histories with scientific fact, this inspirational and fascinating
> look at growing older is highly recommended.[16]

Snowdon's work with the nuns was also the subject of a *Time* mag-azine cover story in 2009.[17] The work illustrates that creative analyt-ical thinking can reach a very wide audience.

Analytical Thinking Example:
The Simon Hannes Insider Trading Case

Simon Hannes formerly worked as an investment banker for Mac-quarie Bank. Acting under the name "Mark Booth," he bought call options for stock in TNT, a transport firm, for about $90,000. Mac-quarie was an adviser to TNT, and just before he left Macquarie, Hannes had indirect access to information that TNT might be ac-quired. TNT was acquired a couple of days after Hannes bought the options, and he made a profit of over $2 million on the transaction. Hannes cleverly disguised his actions, and it took some creative ana-lytical work by investigators at the Australian Securities and Invest-ments Commission (ASIC) to uncover them.

PROBLEM RECOGNITION AND FRAMING. Irregular trading activity in the options market for a TNT stock was identified in a three-day period prior to the announcement of the acquisition of the company. This announcement produced a 200 times return on the investment in less than three days. Notwithstanding that there were a number of entities and individuals named by market supervisors as having traded in that three-day period, they were not able to identify and locate one of the first traders. They referred the matter to ASIC, the market regulator. Despite the deployment of many investigative resources utilizing traditional manual forensic investigation techniques for three months, ASIC was not able to identify the person(s) behind this early trade. Use of a false identity was accepted as the most likely cause of this failure.

REVIEW OF PREVIOUS FINDINGS. There were no previous findings specifically about this case, since it was an isolated event. However, previous research and experience at ASIC suggested that fraudulent transactions typically took place and could be discovered through networks of people. ASIC had previously developed a process to extract networks from a person, company, or address start point within internal and public databases.

MODELING (VARIABLE SELECTION). The two primary variables in the model were whether a person had access to information about the possible acquisition of TNT, and whether a person had the wherewithal (bank account, money, etc.) to effect a trade, and had made actual bank withdrawals at the time of the relevant transactions.

DATA COLLECTION (MEASUREMENT). Traditional investigative techniques were able to identify person(s) who were, or possibly, in possession of the inside information ("persons in the know").

Similarly, ASIC investigators were able to extract relevant cash withdrawals from financial institutions in the relevant geographies by individuals and organizations ("persons with cash"). From this point, they were able to extract and systematically collect associates five times removed (persons, companies, physical addresses, and assets) from persons in the know and persons with cash, utilizing a network extraction process. This process resulted in an analytic data set containing over 160,000 persons, companies, addresses, assets, and cash withdrawals linked via 1 million connections.

DATA ANALYSIS. The data set contained multiple duplicates. As a result, before taking the next step of the analysis, the investigators decided to merge like entities within the data set (i.e., persons, companies, addresses, and assets that appeared to be the same were joined for the purposes of the analysis). ASIC used in excess of one hundred proprietary algorithms to complete this task. Anthony Viel, then the chief investigator for ASIC on the case, and now a partner for analytics and forensics at Deloitte Australia, commented on the rest of the process: "Once all potential duplicates were merged together, we utilized a shortest-path algorithm to identify associations between persons in the know and the cash withdrawals. We separated connection types into 'hard' and 'soft' associations so that we could refine our results. At first pass we identified 65 potential persons with hard and soft connections 3 steps removed. At second pass we identified 2 potential persons 4 steps removed with only hard connections considered. One of these persons was a false positive in that it was the result of an incorrect merge. The other potential was confirmed to be the person of interest."[18]

RESULTS PRESENTATION AND ACTION. Simon Hannes, the person of interest identified through the network analysis, was approached with a search warrant. Several incriminating items were found in his home, and he was charged with several related crimes. He was tried and convicted by a jury, and the conviction was later upheld on appeal. He served about two and a half years in prison, was assessed a $100,000 fine, and was not allowed to keep the proceeds of his insider trade. Viel continues to use similar techniques in analyzing financial and other types of fraud.

6

Developing Quantitative Analysis Capabilities

How is a person's destiny, or way of life, decided? As Aristotle said a very long while ago, our habits, or what we repeatedly do, make us what we are and become our destiny. This can be expressed by the following flow chart:

Thoughts → Actions → Habits → Character → Destiny

Your usual mode of thinking forms your actions. Your actions lead to your habits. Others decide what you are by what you repeatedly do. Finally, what others think about you is associated with your destiny. The process that leads you to become a proficient quantitative analyst follows a similar pattern, as shown in figure 6-1.

FIGURE 6-1

The process of becoming a proficient quantitative analyst

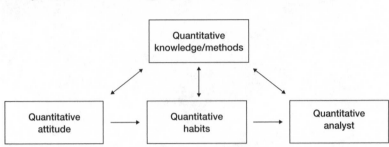

Your usual quantitative attitude forms your quantitative habits. What you repeatedly do with respect to numbers makes you a proficient quantitative analyst. Your quantitative knowledge and methods are gradually improved by interacting with quantitative attitudes and habits. Let's discuss what kinds of quantitative attitude and habits you should have to become a proficient quantitative analyst, and what quantitative knowledge and methods you need to develop at each stage.

Quantitative Attitude

While knowledge of quantitative methods is certainly useful if you want to make analytical decisions, it's just as important to have an attitude that is open to learning about numbers and that insists on a high standard of evidence. If you don't shut your brain down when you see numbers or an equation, you will find that you can master a surprising amount of quantitative analysis.

Don't Be Afraid of Numbers

As we've suggested, innumeracy plagues far too many otherwise knowledgeable people. Many quite "normal" people even have a pathological aversion to math. This is not only unfortunate, but it is unproductive as well. However, math is not the key to good quantitative thinking; what distinguishes good quantitative thinkers is not their skill with pure mathematics, but rather their approach to the classification of quantitative information. Effective quantitative thinkers possess certain attitudes, skills, and habits that they bring to bear whenever they need to make decisions based on numbers. Some experts even assert that the math you learn in elementary school is enough to become a good quantitative thinker: "Mathematical knowledge and quantitative reasoning are quite different things . . . One reason it is so important to underscore the distinction between mathematical knowledge and quantitative reasoning is that being a good quantitative thinker requires very little math beyond sixth-grade levels."[1]

If you don't believe that, take Emily Rosa as an example. She hadn't even made it to sixth grade when, as a nine-year-old, she conducted a mad scientist quantitative analysis on the concept of therapeutic touch. Her work was sufficiently sophisticated and useful to be published in the *Journal of the American Medical Association*.[2] (Published continuously since 1883, JAMA is among the most prestigious medical journals in the world and the most widely circulated.)

How did a fourth-grade science project make it into JAMA? Emily saw her mother, Linda, watching a videotape on a growing industry called *therapeutic touch* (TT), a controversial method of treating ailments by manipulating the patients' "energy fields." Proponents state that more than 100,000 people worldwide have been trained in the TT technique. TT is taught in more than one hundred colleges and universities in seventy-five countries. It is said to be the most recognized technique used by practitioners of holistic nursing. In a TT session, a therapist moves his or her hands just inches away from the patient's body to detect and remove "stagnant energies," which presumably cause various illnesses. Emily suggested to her mother that she might be able to conduct an experiment on such a claim. Linda, who was a nurse, gave Emily some advice on the method. After doing some research, Linda and Emily realized that no previous study attempted to test whether a TT practitioner could actually detect a human energy field.

Emily simply focused on that basic question: if the therapists could do what they claimed, then they must, at least, be able to feel the energy field. If they could not do that, then the medical value of TT would be doubtful. Therefore, if the percentage rate at which the practitioners correctly feel the energy field is not considerably higher than that which could be explained by chance alone, the claims of therapeutic touch are groundless.

By searching for advertisements and following other leads, Emily located twenty-five TT practitioners in northeastern Colorado, twenty-one of whom agreed to be tested. The therapists were informed that the study would be published as her fourth-grade science-fair project. During each test, the therapists rested their hands, palms up, on a flat surface, approximately 25–30 cm apart. To prevent the experimenter's hands from being seen, a tall, opaque screen with cutouts at its base was placed over the subject's arms, and a towel was attached to the screen and draped over the arms.

Emily flipped a coin to determine which of the subject's hands would be the target (known as *randomized assignment to groups* in the quantitative testing field). She then hovered her right hand, palm down, 8–10 cm above the target and said, "Okay." The therapist then stated which of his or her hands was nearer to the experimenter's hand. Two hundred and eighty individual attempts were made by the twenty-one therapists.

Although all of the participants had asserted that they would be able to do this, the therapists correctly located Emily's hand only 122 (44 percent) out of 280 trials, which is no better than would be expected by guessing (see the website for this book). A score of 50 percent would be expected through chance alone. Emily concluded that the therapists' failure to substantiate TT's most fundamental principle is indisputable evidence that the claims of TT are groundless and that further professional use is unjustified. In April 1998, Emily, then eleven years old (and by then actually in the sixth grade), had her experiment published in *JAMA*. George Lundberg, the editor of the journal, said that *JAMA*'s statisticians were amazed by its simplicity and by the clarity of its results.[3] Emily earned her place in the *Guinness Book of World Records* as the youngest person ever to have research published in a major scientific journal.

Emily isn't a genius or child prodigy; she just used good sense and clear quantitative thinking. The most important ability needed to be a proficient quantitative analyst is to extract information from data: a feat based not on mathematical knowledge, but on quantitative thinking. The first step in this direction is to overcome the fear of numbers and to feel comfortable when you encounter them. Have confidence in the knowledge that you already possess the necessary mathematical knowledge, or that you can easily pick up the knowledge you need. The basic DNA to becoming a proficient quantitative analyst is becoming friendly with data, and not having fear.

Even if you got a poor start in math in school, you can always recover; you are not condemned to a nonqualitative perspective throughout life. The fact that you may have gotten off track in the math curriculum doesn't mean that you can't learn what you need later in your career. For example, DJ Patil, who coined the term *data scientist* to describe his role while leading the analytics function at the business networking company LinkedIn, had a disastrous set of school math experiences until later in life: "The first math class I failed was in eighth grade. I progressively kept failing my math classes through high school so I barely graduated, then petitioning to get into the next level and then failing that one. I couldn't get into college so

I went to the local junior college . . . I signed up for calculus there, so I could transfer into the UC system. I went in there and realized, I don't know any of this stuff. I had been in the stupid math classes," he says. "I decided this was ridiculous and I'd like to go to college."[4]

Patil checked out some books from the library and, over a single weekend, taught himself high school math. He did well in calculus and was admitted to UC San Diego, where he finished the math curriculum in three years. Then he began studying for a PhD in applied mathematics at the University of Maryland.

Again, he had some initial difficulty: "I was one of the American-trained students, competing against the Russians, the Israelis, the Koreans. I horribly failed my first qualifier; I think I was the second-lowest score, and the lowest score was someone who didn't show up."

The next time he took the qualifying exam, he got the highest score. Patil eventually graduated and became a faculty member at Maryland, and worked on modeling the complexity of weather. He then worked for the US government on intelligence issues. Research funding was limited at the time, so he left to work for Skype, then owned by eBay. He next became the leader of data scientists at LinkedIn, where the people in that highly analytical position have been enormously influential in product development.

Now Patil is a data scientist in residence (perhaps the first person with that title as well) at the venture capital firm Greylock Partners, helping the firm's portfolio companies to think about data and analytics. He's perhaps the world's best example of latent math talent.

Use a Search Engine to Find the Concepts
Related to Numbers That You Don't Know

In this era of globalization, many economic terms, business terms, and numbers come up in the news every day. The same is true in conversations. Because many people are not familiar with some or most of those terms and numbers, they generally just let them slide and move on. Those aiming to become quantitative analysts, however, should always memorize or jot down those terms and numbers, and Google them later to clearly understand what they mean. There are Wikipedia entries, online courses, and online textbooks galore. Print your search results and make a categorized file for future review. This is a good opportunity to learn and gradually overcome the fear you might have about numbers. You probably won't understand everything you read, but you will be learning nonetheless. If you keep doing this for at least six months, you will be very surprised to find that your friends and colleagues think you a well-informed person, especially when it comes to numbers.

Extend Your Curiosity

When you are curious about numbers, your understanding of them deepens and your knowledge increases considerably. For example, when you find out that the fastest man in the world is Usain Bolt of Jamaica, you might be curious about his best time. You find out that his hundred-meter best time is 9.58 seconds. Then ask yourself how fast it is kilometers per hour or miles per hour. With simple jotting down you will find:

$$9.58 \text{ seconds} \approx 10 \text{ seconds} = \frac{1}{6} \text{ minute} = \frac{1}{360} \text{ hour}$$

$$100 \text{ m} = 0.1 \text{ km}$$

$$\text{Thus, } \frac{0.1 \text{ km}}{\frac{1}{360} \text{ hour}} = 36 \text{ kph} = 22.4 \text{ mph}$$

Now you become inquisitive about the record for the marathon, which is 2:3:59. With simple calculations you learn that this record represents an average speed of over 20.4 kph (12.7 mph). Comparing these two average speeds, you can understand how fast a human can run in both the shortest and longest standard Olympic races.

Curiosity about all aspects of numbers is the hallmark of a good quantitative analyst.

Quantitative Attitudes ⟷ Quantitative Knowledge

To develop quantitative knowledge at this stage, you need to read books that present an introduction to statistics for the general reader. One of the most popular books is Darrell Huff's *How to Lie with Statistics,* the best-selling statistics book of the second half of the twentieth century.[5] This book is a brief, breezy, illustrated volume outlining common errors, both intentional and unintentional, associated with the interpretation of statistics, and how these errors can lead to inaccurate conclusions. It is an excellent text that informs both how others will lie using statistics, and how to interpret the validity of purported statistical data. *Flaws and Fallacies in Statistical Thinking* by Stephen K. Campbell, published in 1974, is still quite useful given the publication date, for anyone who reads newspapers and magazines and comes across statistics there.[6] A modern book by a consulting statistician on the same topic is *Common Errors in Statistics and How to Avoid Them* by Phillip Good and James Hardin.[7] There are plenty of these kinds of books out there. Do an Internet search for popular titles, read some of the reviews, and select several to buy.

Thinking Probabilistically

A key aspect of thinking quantitatively is understanding the laws of probability and randomness. The lack of this understanding is one of the greatest intellectual shortcomings of most adults; as Nassim Nicholas Taleb refers to it in his book of the same name, they are "fooled by randomness"—they impute cosmic significance to events that could easily happen randomly.[8] There is, for example, the "common birthday at a party" misunderstanding. At a birthday party with only twenty-three people present, two attendees discover that they have the same birthday. "What are the chances?" they might comment.

It turns out that the chances are pretty good—just over 50 percent, in fact (see http://keeping upwiththequants.weebly.com).

An understanding of probability is extremely useful not only for understanding birthday parties, but also a variety of human endeavors. If you don't understand probability, you won't understand that the stock market is a *random walk* (that is, changes in stock prices involve no discernable pattern or trend) and that some stock pickers are likely to do better than average for a number of years in a row, but then inevitably crash to earth. You won't understand the *regression to the mean* phenomenon; if your income is well above average, for example, your child's income is likely to be less than yours. You will probably lose a lot of money if you don't understand probability and you frequent the casinos in Las Vegas. You'll have a tough time getting a job in the insurance industry or determining whether and when you should buy an annuity. And, of course, probability is the basis of inferential statistics. In short, you need to understand probability not only to be a quantitative thinker, but to lead a successful life.

There are, of course, many sources of learning about probability. Most textbooks pair the topic with basic statistics, because statistics requires probabilistic thinking. The books we mentioned earlier in this chapter have some sections on probability. If you want to focus on probability and not statistics in general, an introductory textbook on probability is Richard Isaac's *The Pleasures of Probability*.[9] If you can't tolerate a textbook, a fun and well-written introduction for the general reader is Leonard Mlodinow's *The Drunkard's Walk: How Randomness Rules Our Lives*.[10]

Going Back to School

You don't have to be self-taught about analytics, probability, and quantitative thinking if you don't want to be. There are a variety of sources of education, both online and face-to-face. Universities are increasingly making course materials available online for free, and there are a variety of statistics courses among them. For example, if you want to learn from one of the most quantitatively oriented universities in the world, you can click over to an MIT course in probability and statistics.[11] In terms of online education you pay for, you can buy (for a little over a hundred bucks) from Harvard Business Publishing (the publishers of this book) a self-paced course in quantitative methods taught by Tom's colleague at Harvard Business School, Jan Hammond. Or if you want to spend considerably more money, you can get a master's of science in predictive analytics degree entirely from online courses at Northwestern University.

If you like to see professors face-to-face, talk with them easily, and learn from face-to-face interaction with your peers, there are a growing number of analytics degree programs—most granting master's degrees—at US universities. The granddaddy of them all—because it was founded five years ago—and one of the most well designed of such programs is the Master of Science in Analytics (MSA) at North Carolina State University.[12] Why NC State? Well, Jim Goodnight, the CEO and founder of analytics software company SAS, was a student there and taught there, and he generously donated the money to found the program.

The MSA is a professional program that focuses on a thorough understanding of the tools, methods, applications, and practice of advanced analytics. Its design principles are, we think, well suited to the topic and the need for quantitatively focused people in businesses and organizations:

- *Quick to complete:* Ten months of intensive study—three semesters (summer, fall, spring); enroll in July, graduate the following May; no part-time learning.

- *A demanding course of study:* Full-time (M–F/9–5) study on campus; an integrated curriculum shared with the other students; working in teams throughout the program; and, typically, working on projects when not in class

- *A broad and practical content focus:* An integrated, multidisciplinary curriculum (drawing from multiple schools and departments at NC State) aimed at the acquisition of practical skills which can be applied to real-world problems, drawing on fields such as statistics, applied mathematics, computer science, operations research, finance and economics, and marketing science

- *Learning by doing:* Use of a practicum rather than the traditional MS thesis (students work in teams of five individuals, then use real-world problems and data provided by an industry sponsor; highly structured, substantive work conducted over seven months culminates in a final report to the sponsor)

The NCSU MSA has a novel curriculum consisting of classes developed exclusively for the program. Topics include data mining, text mining, forecasting, optimization, databases, data visualization, data privacy and security, financial analytics, and customer analytics.

Students come into the program with a variety of backgrounds, though some degree of quantitative orientation is desired. The average age of students is twenty-seven, and about 26 percent of students enrolled have a prior graduate degree. About half the students were previously employed full time. Despite an uncertain economy and the slow growth in domestic employment, the MSA class of 2011 logged a record 469 job interviews (an average of twelve for each of its forty students—increasing to eighty in 2012–2013). The program has had 100 percent job placement for five straight years. Considering that employers' demand for MSA graduates has been increasing, it is natural that this type of degree program will be opened at other universities as well. SAS has sponsored new programs at Louisiana State and Texas A&M. The University of San Francisco has created a West Coast program as well, and New York University has begun one in New York. One recent survey found that fifty-nine universities were offering either degrees or majors in business analytics or business intelligence—thirty-seven at the masters level and twenty-two undergraduate programs.[13] Schools are also beginning to offer courses in data science, and degree programs will follow soon.

Quantitative Habits

Attitudes are important, but so are habits. It has often been said that it is easier to act your way into a new way of thinking than to think your way into a new way of acting. If you practice the following quantitative habits, you'll eventually find that you've developed a quantitative attitude.

Demand Numbers

Good quantitative thinkers (and organizations that want to nourish them) should always demand numbers when someone presents ideas, hunches, theories, and casual observations. Practice the question, "Do you have data to support that hypothesis?" If you are really brave, you might practice the phrase, "The plural of anecdote is not data." Demanding this data is important because it answers the following questions: How is this person thinking? Via what processes, and assisted by what tools, was this course of action reached? In addition to straightening out the rest of the world, suppress your own impulses to jump to conclusions without quantified data.

The same is also true when you present your ideas to others. If no data exists, do a little mad scientist experiment to gather some. You should have the urge to seek hard data before you fully develop your theories. By doing so, you can solidify your ideas with careful quantitative analyses and increase your chances of persuading others with your ideas. The habits of demanding numbers and concluding your ideas with numbers are an indispensable gene to becoming a proficient quantitative analyst.

Never Trust Numbers

We've just said you should always try to gather numbers and other data to support your theories and views of the world. Now we're going to tell you to be suspicious of them. Just as with a new acquaintance, don't trust data until you know more about it. You should never take at face value any numbers presented to you. There are several reasons why numbers may not be worthy of your trust. People (especially politicians) sometimes lie and cheat with numbers, or at least misinterpret them to advance a hidden agenda. As Scottish poet and critic Andrew Lang put it, "He uses statistics like a drunken man uses a lamp post, more for support than illumination."[14] Numbers can be outdated and thus incorrect now. The numbers may not be a good sample (i.e., not representative of the population someone is attempting to describe). Having a critical perspective toward numbers is appropriate, especially when numbers surprise you and are atypical. The surest way to be confident about any numbers presented to you is to be skeptical of them, and to learn more about their background. More specifically, doubt with regard to numbers should focus on the following three categories.

RELEVANCE. The numbers presented to you should be relevant to the question to which they are applied, and representative of the group or entity they supposedly represent. If the numbers do not give some answer to the question, they are merely meaningless.

ACCURACY. If the numbers are relevant but not accurate, you need to discard them. The accuracy of numbers can be evaluated by questioning who and how they made them. Numbers that do not pass your credibility tests are useless.

CORRECT INTERPRETATION. Even when accurate, numbers can often be misleading if they're misrepresented. Especially people who have an ulterior agenda are apt to mislead with numbers intentionally. Let's look at an example where the same number was interpreted in a manner that best supports prejudices:

> The *Newsweek* critic who reviewed a book, called *The Better Half,* about the early suffragettes, ended his critique on a thought-provoking note. He wondered rhetorically what Susan B. Anthony and the other suffragettes would have said about the fact that almost 50 years after the enfranchisement of American women, a Columbia University sociologist found that only one wife in 22 said she cast a different vote from her husband.
>
> A reader wrote saying, "I feel that they would have been quite pleased. The feminist movement must have come a long way, if after fewer than 50 years since the enfranchisement of American women, only one husband out of 22 has the courage to vote against his wife."[15]

In sum, you should always question whether the numbers presented to you are appropriately interpreted with respect to the problem at hand.

Be Particularly Suspicious of Causation Arguments

One of the most important things to be skeptical about in analytical reasoning involves the difficulty of establishing causation. As we mentioned earlier in describing mad scientist experiments, if you create test and control groups and randomly assign people to them, if there turns out to be a difference in outcomes between the two groups, you can usually attribute it to being caused by the test condition. But if you simply find a statistical relationship between two factors, it's unlikely to be a causal relationship. You may have heard the phrase, "correlation is not causation," and it's important to remember.

Cognitive psychologists Christopher Chabris and Daniel Simons suggest a useful technique for checking on the causality issue in their book *The Invisible Gorilla and Other Ways Our Intuitions Deceive Us*: "When you hear or read about an association between two factors, think about whether people could have been assigned randomly to conditions for one of them. If it would have been impossible, too expensive, or ethically dubious to randomly assign people to those groups, then the study could not have been an experiment and the causal inference is not supported."[16]

If, for example, you read in the newspaper that "heavy drinking causes cancer in ten-year study," ask yourself whether test subjects would be randomly assigned to groups and asked to either drink heavily or not drink at all for ten years. This seems unlikely. What is more likely is that a researcher found a correlation between heavy drinking (probably self-reported) and cancer in a population that was monitored over ten years. The researcher may well have cautioned that the correlation found could be explained by other variables (the heavy drinkers may also have been heavy smokers, for example), but the newspaper writer didn't.

If you suspect that someone in your organization is employing the *cum hoc ergo propter hoc* (A is correlated with B, therefore A causes B) fallacy, most of the remedies involve either a detailed knowledge of experimental design, or a detailed knowledge of statistics and econometrics. So that might be a good time to call in an expert.

Ask Questions

The reason for asking questions is to understand more clearly both the problem and the process. Likewise, when you have doubts about the numbers presented, you should ask questions without any hesitation. Many people are reluctant to ask questions about numbers because they're afraid of appearing foolish; this fear is exaggerated. For some ideas about what questions to ask, see "Good Questions About Quantitative Analyses."

Imagine that someone asks a question about the numbers presented—that person would probably seem courageous and respectable rather than stupid. So, if you come across a number you don't understand, feel free to ask a question. Moreover, for some numbers, a follow-up question should be anticipated. For example, when you are presented with an average, you should ask about the dispersion of the distribution, or the standard deviation. You could also ask about whether there are any outliers in the data that might be the result of errors or oddities, or any missing data that might be significant. You might ask what the median is if you are presented with a mean. Interpreting an average without knowing its dispersion can be quite misleading because the individual observations may differ substantially one from another. Also, when someone talks about numbers from a certain survey, you should ask who performed the survey, how it was created, and with what kind of question wording. Talking about survey results without answers to these questions will lead to wrong conclusions. In short, you should get into the habit of questioning and probing, because doing so is an important part of building your quantitative skills.

Practice Quantitative Analyses

Like the young man who asked someone how to get to Carnegie Hall in New York, if you want to develop the art, skill, and discipline of

Good Questions About Quantitative Analyses

The questions in the following list are certainly not all the possible questions you could ask, but they should get you started. They work for almost any quantitative analysis, or nonquantitative analysis that should be quantitative.

1. Do you have any data to support that hypothesis?

2. Can you tell me something about the source of data you used in your analysis?

3. Are you sure that the sample data are representative of the population?

4. Are there any outliers in your data distribution? How did they affect the results?

5. What assumptions are behind your analysis?

6. Are there conditions that would make your assumptions and your model invalid?

7. Can you tell me why you decided on that particular approach to analysis?

8. What transformations did you have to do to the data to get your model to fit well?

9. Did you consider any other approaches to analyzing the data, and if so why did you reject them?

10. How likely do you think it is that the independent variables are actually causing the changes in the dependent variable? Are there more analyses that could be done to get a better idea of causality?

quantitative analysis, you should "practice, practice, practice." At first you may struggle in making progress on one problem. However, struggling is a natural phase in learning and only through struggle can you improve your analytical capabilities—slowly but steadily. You can work on your own analytical capabilities in the same six-step way we've described for solving a particular problem:

- *Problem recognition:* You probably have many issues at work. Prioritize them according to urgency and the applicability of quantitative analyses beginning at the top of the list. The most important thing in the problem recognition stage is to fully understand what the problem is and why it matters. The answers to these two questions not only make it clear what can be accomplished by solving the problem, but also facilitate the ensuing stages.

- *Review of previous findings:* Once the problem is recognized, all the previous findings connected to the problem should be investigated. Although you have to spend considerable time at this stage, making the best of search engines like Google can be very helpful. Searching through problem-related knowledge is very important in getting to the bottom of the problem, as is identifying relevant variables and seizing on a general association from among the identified variables. Once you have a comprehensive grasp of the previous findings, you will gain a clearer picture of how to solve the problem. You can put it like this: "Question is well defined; all previous findings reviewed: more than half done."

- *Modeling (variable selection):* If you have identified all the relevant variables by reviewing the previous findings, begin to throw away, one by one, all variables that are not directly relevant to the solution of the problem. Which variables to throw away and which to keep depends mainly on the purpose of the model. If you want to make a toy train, then the scale of an actual train matters. In contrast, if you need to calculate the economic feasibility of a train, then variables like tonnage hauled, speed, and fuel consumption become very relevant. When you practice concentrating on certain features of a problem as if drawing a caricature, you are getting nearer to the solution and your quantitative perspectives improve.

- *Data collection (measurement):* To measure the selected variables, you should first check whether the data is already collected by others in your organization. In many cases the variables at hand have been measured and accumulated either in another department, or even your own. You may even find that the data is publicly available. Even if you have to buy it, it's almost always cheaper than gathering your own. When data directly relevant to your problem is not available, carefully choose what method to use to collect it. If you decide to use a survey, the specific design and even the wording of a questionnaire should be scrupulously studied. If you decide to do an experiment to gather data, make sure you consult a specialist in experimental design. Because obtaining accurate and timely data is very important to solving the problem, sufficient time and effort need to be invested at this stage.

- *Data analysis:* Data analysis consists of finding consistent patterns, or the relationships among the variables. The type of statistical method to use is decided at the problem recognition step: when you come to fully understand what the problem is, which method to choose in the succeeding data analysis stage becomes apparent. If it is the problem of comparison between groups, you need to use the relevant technique. If it is the problem of dependence between variables, a regression or similar method should be used. As these techniques are popularly used in many situations, you need to spend enough time to get used to the concepts and applications of those techniques. And there are probably experts in your organization who could offer you advice.

- *Results presentation and action:* Don't neglect practicing this all-important piece of quantitative thinking. Successful analytical groups devote as much time to this step as to the previous five. Talk with others in your organization about how they communicate analytical results, and discuss some of your own ideas on that topic with them. And learn the language of graphic display of statistics—make the books of Edward Tufte your friends, for example. And if Tufte comes to your city with one of his one-day "Presenting Data and Information" courses, don't miss it.

Quantitative Habits ⟷ Quantitative Knowledge/Methods

At this phase you need to study the basics to understand and apply quantitative analyses. The courses you have to master first are Elementary Statistics and Research Methods. It would be great if you can take these courses on line. You can also learn in stages through the Internet or textbooks whenever you run into certain concepts. Many people experience difficulties understanding the concepts in elementary statistics because many textbooks do not elaborate how the concepts are applied to real-world problems. Therefore you need to carefully select a text that introduces you to practical statistics application rather than theory only. Consequently, we recommend

Heinz Kohler's *Statistics for Business and Economics* as your main text.[17] As one reviewer commented on Amazon.com:

> Best Stats Learning Book Ever.
>
> I was scared to death about the upcoming statistics course . . . I had the feeling that it would be very difficult for me to learn about the concepts and inference in statistics . . . The layouts and the structure in the chapters are so easy to follow . . . Statistics never became a problem for me! I was amazed how easy Kohler made statistics a very interesting and easy subject.[18]

The same goes for research methods; there are also plenty of textbooks on this subject. Go online and read some of the reviews before you choose a text. The most important thing in studying these basic courses is to try to solve all the exercise questions in the books. Since most of these questions are designed to link theories to practice, you can firmly grasp the concepts you are learning through the exercises. If you read the selected texts thoroughly at least three times, then you will almost master all the basic knowledge you need to be a proficient quantitative analyst. Now what you have to do is to practice (practice, practice).

The Quantitative Analyst

In business, the activities included in quantitative analysis take place in a process and a social context. They typically include not only doing the analysis, but also writing a report (or giving a presentation) about it, working with other analysts in a community, learning from each other in activities like seminars, and working with experts. These activities are critical to developing analytical skills.

Write a Report

The first step toward practice is to write a report, which helps you learn how to "tell a story with data." You will probably learn a lot from reading texts, but you will learn a great deal more if you scrupulously try to solve a real problem and then write a follow-up report. It would be impressive if you were to choose a problem that is mind-boggling to many people at your organization, but don't worry if it isn't. Pay close attention to selecting the right problem, since, as Voltaire said, people judge you by your questions, rather than by your answers. Then scrupulously follow the six-step framework of quantitative analysis and use the formal report to present your findings and suggestions. Writing a report has three purposes:

- You will learn more and improve your analytical proficiency by completing a real problem on your own.

- You can make a serious contribution to solving the problem at work.

- You can help to create an analytical atmosphere at work and motivate others to think and act analytically.

Do not expect too much from your first attempt, but make sure that your report proves the following: that you critically reviewed all the previous findings, that you exerted more effort than anyone else to solve the problem, and that your work is analytically stringent. Remember that you will also be judged by the way you tried to solve the question, and not just by your conclusions.

Form a Quantitative Analysis Community

Find a friend or group of coworkers to form a committee for quantitative analysis. There are many good reasons for forming a committee: to study together effectively, to work on projects efficiently, and to play a pivotal role in promoting analytical approaches at work. In the club, you can set up a priority hierarchy for challenges at work, discuss the issues, divide tasks according to the six-step framework, explain what you worked on, and take turns making presentations to one another. This kind of group setting is the surest and fastest way to learn. As Henry Ford said, "Coming together is a beginning. Keeping together is progress. Working together is success." Also, this small group of analytically oriented employees could change the company, especially by creating an analytical atmosphere and motivating others to think and act analytically as well.

Hold Seminars Regularly

The purposes of seminars are obvious: to have an opportunity to present the results of the committee members' projects and discuss with appropriate people at work, to expedite future projects, and to further extend an atmosphere for analytics and fact-based decision making. Many companies also bring in external speakers on analytical topics. A regular and focused seminar usually gives all participants informative and inspiring experiences and motivates them to exceed their current performance for subsequent seminars. Try to make some of them accessible to nontechnical people.

Quantitative Analyst ⟷ Quantitative Knowledge/Methods

At this stage, the main focus of group study is to learn by analyzing how quantitative analyses are done for various real-world problems. You can start with the cases presented in this book. Prepare the original papers or materials, take turns making presentations to one another, and discuss the details within the six-step framework. When an advanced quantitative method appears, this is a good chance to learn it together in a real application setting. Also, inviting a specialist to explain the method in detail, and to discuss strengths of and caveats associated with the technique, can be very helpful. You may well be able to find such a specialist in your own company, or at least at a local university.

If you take all or many of the steps described in this chapter, you will be well on your way to being at least a semiprofessional quantitative analyst. You will have undoubtedly improved your career prospects and expanded your mind. And you'll be an integral part of a major transformation in business and organizational life that is sweeping the world right now.

Analytical Thinking Example: Scholarship Made Easy

In academia, the competition for tenure-track faculty positions puts increasing pressure on scholars to publish new work frequently. The phrase "publish-or-perish" well represents, especially in prestigious and research-oriented universities, the pressure to publish work constantly to further or sustain a career in higher education. However, since preparing work for publication in a journal, especially in major journals, is not easy and takes copious amounts of time, working with other scholars is more productive and has become the prevalent path to publication. Collaboration between professors and graduate students is also common. The key, then, to receiving a scholarship to graduate school is to be prepared enough, or to possess sufficient research capabilities, to assist professors in their work.

Jinho lives in South Korea and has two daughters studying in the United States. By himself, he cannot afford to send two daughters to study there, but he did a systematic analysis on how to guarantee a graduate school scholarship. Now his two daughters are fellowship students in the PhD programs of Stanford and the University of Michigan, respectively. At first, Jinho was hesitant to discuss his family's story, but decided to go ahead to show how students with quantitative backgrounds can get scholarships with ease, and how thinking intentionally and systematically about your quantitative analysis skills pays off.

When Jinho's elder daughter, Nuri, was a senior in college, she wanted to complete her studies in America. She knew it was imperative to get a scholarship in order to study abroad. However, obtaining a scholarship is very difficult for a foreign student with a major in communications. Jinho encouraged her by advising her that it would not be that difficult if she was well prepared. Nuri followed his lead and prepared to apply for scholarships.

So what kind of preparation is needed to persuade graduate admission committee members that Nuri is capable of assisting their research, and thereby worthy of a scholarship? Let's draw the six steps of quantitative analysis and discuss both the leading roles of professors and the assisting ones of their graduate students (see figure 6-2).

FIGURE 6-2

Does Nuri qualify for a scholarship? Six steps of a quantitative analysis

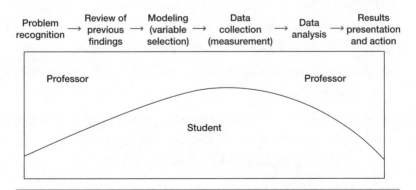

A typical activity in the problem recognition stage is to determine a research topic that has a high chance of being accepted in a journal. Professors usually play a leading role in this stage. The review of previous findings stage should prove how this new research topic differs from existing studies and can contribute uniquely to existing knowledge. Professors are also expected to play a main role in this step.

Professors normally determine what data are to be collected. Graduate students normally assist professors in the data collection and data analysis stages. These tasks are normally relegated to graduate students because they are relatively labor and time intensive. Thus, the surest way to get a scholarship is first to be able to understand why a specific topic is selected and how it will be researched; second, to show that you are good at collecting data and analyzing them under a professor's supervision. Finally, professors normally write the article for journal submission after the graduate students collect and manipulate the data.

To prepare for the scholarship application process, Nuri took both introductory statistics and research methods classes. To further deepen her understanding of the concepts, Jinho and Nuri had Q&A and discussion sessions for each chapter of her textbooks. She also took an intensive program on the use of SPSS (a statistical package) to accustom herself to analyzing data. Finally, Jinho and Nuri read together twenty recent articles published in some major communication journals and critically discussed the ideas of the papers, research methods, data collections, data analyses, and results interpretation. This process was needed for Nuri to get a clear understanding of how the concepts she learned in the three preparation courses applied to actual research settings. All preparations were completed during Nuri's senior year. Her research capabilities at the end of this year were such that she was qualified and ready to support any professor's research.

Nuri detailed her preparations and abilities in the "Statement of Purpose" in her master's programs applications and won a scholarship from the University of Wisconsin. There, thanks to her preparation, Nuri worked with several professors to publish various papers. Later she received a fellowship from Stanford University, and she is now busy writing her PhD thesis. Youngri, Jinho's younger daughter, after following the same steps as her sister, received a fellowship from the University of Michigan. She is working in the chemical engineering laboratory.

Analytical Thinking Example: Daryl Morey and Shane Battier of the Houston Rockets

This example is about two quantitatively oriented people in the field of professional basketball. Daryl Morey is the general manager of the NBA Houston Rockets. For those who are familiar with the book and movie *Moneyball,* Morey has a good claim on the title of "the Billy Beane of professional basketball."[19] He was a computer science and statistics major in college at Northwestern, and received an MBA from the MIT Sloan School of Management. He always had the goal of applying Bill James's ideas about baseball statistics to other professional sports, and he became the senior vice president of Operations and Information for the Boston Celtics. At thirty-five, he became general manager of the Rockets and proceeded to employ a variety of statistical and quantitative methods to improve the team's performance. He is also chair of the annual MIT Sports Analytics Conference, which now attracts over two thousand attendees.

Shane Battier is an NBA player—a forward—who currently plays for the Miami Heat. He played for the Houston Rockets from 2006 to 2011. He is relatively analytical as professional basketball players go, and was named the seventh-smartest player in professional sports by *Sporting News* magazine.[20] Daryl Morey notes (in an article by *Moneyball* author Michael Lewis) that Battier was

> ... given his special package of information. "He's the only player we give it to," Morey says. "We can give him this fire hose of data and let him sift. Most players are like golfers. You don't want them swinging while they're thinking." The data essentially broke down the floor into many discrete zones and calculated the odds of Bryant making shots from different places on the court, under different degrees of defensive pressure, in different relationships to other players—how well he scored off screens, off pick-and-rolls, off catch-and-shoots and so on. Battier learns a lot from studying the data on the superstars he is usually assigned to guard.[21]

Battier, however, was a controversial player for the Rockets, which the six-step framework indicates.

PROBLEM RECOGNITION AND FRAMING. Should the Rockets acquire Battier as a player, even though his individual performance statistics (points scored, rebounds, etc.) were not impressive?

REVIEW OF PREVIOUS FINDINGS. Sports analytics are increasingly common, and there are many books (and even more websites) on the topic today. Yet such analysis is much easier in sports where players' individual performance statistics are highly relevant to team success. In basketball, the dynamics of overall team performance and player interaction are more difficult to measure. Battier had relatively weak performance numbers at the individual level (in five years playing for the Memphis Grizzlies out of college, he averaged just over 10 points per game, and just under five rebounds per game). However, his team and fellow players seemed to perform better—sometimes much better—when he was in the game.

MODELING (VARIABLE SELECTION). The variables in deciding whether to acquire Battier from the Grizzlies would be the cost of acquiring him (outright or in trade for other players), the amount that he would be paid going forward, various individual performance measures, and ideally some measure of team performance while Battier was on the court versus when he was not.

DATA COLLECTION (MEASUREMENT). The individual performance metrics and financials were easy to gather. And there is a way to measure an individual player's impact on team performance. The "plus/minus" statistic, adapted by Roland Beech of *82games.com* from a similar statistic used in hockey, compares how a team performs with a particular player in the game versus its performance when he is on the bench.

DATA ANALYSIS. Morey and his statisticians decided to use plus/minus analysis to evaluate Battier. There are various versions of the plus/minus statistic that are adjusted (using regression analysis) for a variety of factors, including the quality of a player's teammates and the opponents he played against. We don't know exactly how Morey computed the statistic to acquire Battier. But in the 2006–2007 season, his first with the Rockets, Morey said that Battier had an adjusted plus/minus of 8, meaning that if he were replaced by an average NBA player, the Rockets' point differential versus other teams would have decreased by 8 points.[22] Battier ranked seventeenth in the NBA on this statistic, yet he had an average salary level for the league, and the player he was traded for was ranked 45th in plus/minus.

RESULTS PRESENTATION AND ACTION. Morey did, of course, make the trade for Battier, and felt that he performed well for the Rockets. The season before Battier arrived, the Rockets finished 34-48. In the 2007–2008 season with the Rockets, the team finished 52-30, and in 2008–2009 had a record of 55-27—a stretch of twenty-two straight wins, many games of which the Rockets' best-known players were hurt. Battier played for five years for the Rockets until he was hurt and traded back to the Grizzlies, and then joined the Heat. Battier also performed well for Miami (in his typically unobtrusive fashion), and the team won the NBA championship in 2012.

7

Working with Quants

Since this book is for non-quants, we thought it would be useful to describe how you can best deal with analytical professionals and data scientists. Even though you will have learned a lot by reading this book and by doing some of the knowledge-building activities suggested in the previous chapter, it won't be enough for you to do sophisticated analytics by yourself. You'll have to occasionally work with specialists in quantitative fields. Quantitative analysts and data scientists often have PhDs or master's degrees in quantitative fields like statistics, math, and even physics. That tells you something about the level of quant skills necessary to do serious work.

What we are primarily describing in this chapter is a set of relationships between three sets of players:

- Business or organizational decision makers

- Business professionals or team members

- Quantitative analysts or data scientists

Our assumption in this book is that you are in one of the first two categories and need to work closely with people in the third category. If you are in the third category, you may also find this chapter useful, as it will give you some guidance as to how to work effectively with non-quants.

There is a good reason for a mutual accommodation of these three groups, rather than one of them turning things over fully to another. We are, if you haven't noticed this far in the book, big advocates of analytics and data as a basis for decision making. However, intuition and experience are still important decision resources for many executives. They can lead to bias in decisions, but they are undeniably helpful in establishing the appropriate financial metrics, proposing crucial "what-if" business scenarios, and setting the conditions for which analytical models are relevant.

The goal, then, is to make analytical decisions while preserving the role of the executive's gut. Few executives are skilled at both analytics and intuition. This means that they will need to work closely with quantitative analysts if they are going to be effective decision makers. In fact, we would argue that the quality of relationships between executives and their quantitatively oriented advisers is a key factor in effective decision making.

As Karl Kempf, an Intel Fellow (one of those roles for distinguished scientific types who have earned a lot of autonomy in their work) who heads a decision engineering group at the company puts it, effective quantitative decisions "are not about the math; they're about the relationships."[1] This is a notable statement from Kempf, who is known informally around Intel as the "UberQuant" and the "Chief Mathematician." If someone referred to as the Chief Mathematician declares that it's not about the math, we should pay attention.

Kempf has observed that the mathematical and statistical algorithms that quantitative analysts apply when performing analytics can be very simple or staggeringly complex. But in all cases the algorithms have resulted from the very careful work of very smart people over decades (or centuries, as we have noted in some of our examples) and have been checked, cross-checked, and dissected over and over by other very smart people.

The math works, but the human side of these decisions is typically much less refined. Organizations that maintain quantitative analyst groups—and all should in this analytical age—need to carefully address the types of analysts they hire and the roles they play relative to executives. Analysts with the right combination of skills are likely to be in short supply. In addition, executives need to change their expectations of, and relationships with, analysts. Finally, the methods and tools that such quantitative groups employ need to be expanded and refined to seamlessly integrate with how people and organizations really make decisions.

Business-Quant Relationships in Decision Engineering at Intel

Karl Kempf and his analytical team at Intel have observed firsthand many of the lessons we describe in this section. The group is highly focused on relationships between analysts and decision makers. It strives to find ways to build mutual respect—to get the business decision maker to have a little interest and respect for the skills of the quantitative analyst, and to get the math person to have a big interest and a lot of respect for the insights of the business decision maker. The asymmetry in the relationship is intentional. While it is good for the business decision maker to get a bit of a feel for the math, Kempf and his group feel it is absolutely vital for the math person to get as deep an understanding of the intuition of the business person as possible. This does not equate to the decision maker becoming a math expert, but it may equate to the math person becoming a business expert.

While the math person can never fully understand the origins of the business intuition—by definition—the math person must understand what the intuition is and speak the language of the business person. Intel's approach is to send one of its "math people" off into the business—at least to listen, learn, and after a suitable time, ask questions. At most, the analyst can be trained, as a new hire would be, to participate in the business process. In both cases the mission is to understand the formal and informal organization, how the group is incentivized and rewarded, and so forth.

Kempf judges the low bar for success as when the math person thinks he or she understands the business problem. The high bar is when the business person thinks the math person understands the business problem. This generally builds some business respect for the math person ("first time anyone has actually come and spent time to understand our problems—this person is genuinely interested in helping us"), and very often builds some math respect for the business person ("not as easy as I thought it would be—this guy is actually pretty clever").

Assuming the greatest advocate of employing analytics made it possible for the math person to temporarily observe or join the business group, a useful side goal here is to identify and engage the biggest naysayers in the group. In the worst case they may be right, and it can't be done; in the best case you already know the most important candidates to critique demonstrations of results or solutions. Anne Robinson, who has led an analytics group at Cisco Systems and now does so at Verizon Wireless, also emphasizes the importance of incorporating skeptics into the list of stakeholders. "They keep you honest and keep the team high-performing," she says. "If you can convince them, you can convince anybody." (We describe an example of Anne's work at Cisco at the end of this chapter.)

At Intel, the next step in the relationship is for decision makers and quants to collaborate to build the basic model. The key quant person drives these brainstorms to elicit inputs (data elements, sources of data, ideas for detecting and fixing bad data), outputs (what solution slices and dices are most desirable, what display methods are most intuitively satisfying to the intended business users), what are the key variables, and what are the key relationships between variables.

Again, in such exercises, the business person doesn't have to understand, for example, hyperbolic partial differential equations, but at minimum there has to be a diagram on the white board setting out such questions as:

- Since A and X are related, if A goes up, in what direction does X go?

- What are the highest and lowest values key variable B can take?

- If there is a time lag between cause Y and effect Q, how long might it be?

As with any other type of model, a few concrete examples (historical or made up) are extremely useful to step through in structuring the basic model. In this exercise, the quant must listen carefully, ask clarifying questions, and absorb as much of the knowledge of the business decision maker as possible. This is as much about relationship building as it is model building.

At this point the quant team should be ready to spring into action. It needs to select the right math approach, formalize the model so it can be represented in the computer, collect the data, and get it into the computer. The analyst can then test the model by performing sensitivity analysis on variables and relationships, and trying alternatives. When the business decision maker can supply some test problems, the analyst can begin to detect biases in the perceptions of either the decision maker or the analyst and adjust the model appropriately. The most important aspect of this stage is to get a prototype to run as soon as possible and show it to the intended users for feedback. It is usually a good idea to do a couple of rounds of this with different people from the business to test the completeness of the model and the consensus of the business team.

The model and the system are then refined based on feedback and redemonstrated. In other words, it's important to fail early and often. At each round, there will be things the quant forgot, misunderstood, or simply got wrong; and things the business decision makers forget to say, said but don't like now that they see it, and so forth. Whether the project is a one-shot analysis or ongoing use of an analysis tool, success on the problem generally builds success in the relationship. The business decision maker probably needs to have some faith at first, but if things go well, that is quickly replaced by credibility based on experience. The development of mutual trust, respect, and understanding takes effort and time—especially from the analyst, because the business person doesn't have that much time to invest. It is often the case that an initial successful relationship leads to a sequence of powerful analyses and support tools as well as deepening trust and understanding.

The ROI of Combining Art and Science at Intel

The approach just described has been developed and continuously improved over twenty-plus years of projects covering the analytics spectrum at Intel, and it has yielded considerable benefits. Initial work focused on manufacturing, including factory design, construction, ramp-up, and operations. Problems analyzed and decision policies implemented spanned problems from determining machine quantities and layout to managing work-in-progress and equipment maintenance.

A second major body of analytics work focused on integrated production, inventory, and logistics planning across Intel's factory network. With production facilities in the United States, Costa Rica, Ireland, Israel, China, Malaysia, and most recently Vietnam—all operating 24/365—analytics in the factories spanned not only time zones but also cultures and languages.

Subsequent projects looked upstream and downstream in the supply chain. Projects on contract structures for equipment and materials focused on win-win relationships with suppliers and optimizing Intel's agility. Demand forecasting and finished product positioning projects focused on service to customers and containing supply chain costs. These systems continue to be in active use, or have been upgraded by second- and third-generation analysis systems and decision policies. Work has most recently spread into Intel's extensive product development organizations. The decision-engineering analysts are now building relationships with senior business personnel with intuition and experience about future products. Their recent analysis projects run from selecting features for future products to playing out product roadmap scenarios to allocating critical engineering resources to project portfolio management.

These projects and their impact garnered Intel the 2009 Institute for Operations Research and the Management Sciences prize for "repeatedly applied the principles of operations research and the management sciences in pioneering, varied, novel, and lasting ways." In accepting the award, Intel's then chairman of the board Craig Barrett credited the application of advanced analytics with enhancing competitiveness for the previous two decades adding billions (that's with a *b*) of dollars to the bottom line.

Your Analytical Responsibilities

If analytical problem solving is going to take place successfully, there are some specific responsibilities for both quantitative analysts and business decision makers (you). We have spent much of this book describing what quants do and how you can understand their data and reports better. Now it's time to address the analytical roles that businesspeople must play, whether they are mathematically focused or not (see "What Quantitative Analysts Should Expect of Business Decision Makers").

What Quantitative Analysts Should Expect of Business Decision Makers

As a business decision maker, you should:

- Give the analysts enough of your time and attention to ensure that they understand the problem from your perspective

- Make available the time and attention of people within your organization who can help them understand the details of the business situation

- Have a firm understanding of the time and money necessary to build the solution, and jointly agree on this as a proposal

- Learn enough about the underlying math and statistics to have a general idea of how the model works and when it might be invalid

- Politely push back if you don't understand something, and ask for a different or better explanation

- Attend all relevant briefings, demonstrations, and launch meetings

- Let your employees know that using the new model effectively is important to your success, and to theirs

Learning Something About Math and Statistics

In chapter 6, we suggested various ways that businesspeople can learn about statistics. We think that this responsibility extends to businesspeople at every level, including senior executive decision makers. Why? In this data-intensive society and business culture, you simply can't understand how data and analytics can be applied to decision making without some mathematical sophistication.

Those who lack understanding can get into trouble easily, as the Joe Cassano example at AIG Financial Products in chapter 1 illustrates. Many businesses increasingly use statistical and mathematical models in their business operations. Therefore, a key principle is that managers shouldn't build analytical models into their businesses that they don't understand. As Yale economist Robert Shiller puts it (in the context of explaining some of the reasons for the 2008–2009 financial crisis, which he anticipated), "You have to be a quantitative person if you're managing a company. The quantitative details really matter."[2]

Some organizations insist on a familiarity with math and models. Ed Clark, the CEO of TD Bank Group, who has a PhD in economics from Harvard, avoided the problems that many US banks encountered in the financial crisis. He reflected on the problem at other banks in the *Toronto Star:* "What I found frightening was, when I talked to my counterparts in the area [of structured products], I gradually realized that they didn't understand what these products actually were. They had never sat down and gone through the mathematics of the individual products. It's partly because they were delegating too far down in their organizations the understanding of these products."[3]

As all industries become more data oriented and analytical, it is incumbent upon senior executives to master some degree of analytical complexity. Otherwise, they're not going to be able to push back when some trader suggests that they take on inordinate and poorly understood risk, or when a marketer suggests a predictive model that employs too much customer data. Otherwise, they're putting their institutions and their customers in great jeopardy.

Some of the concepts that any executive needs to understand include:

- Measures of central tendency (mean, median, mode)

- Probability and distributions

- Sampling

- The basics of correlation and regression analysis

- The rudiments of experimental design

- The interpretation of visual analytics

The methods for acquiring this knowledge can be the same as for more junior personnel, except that senior executives may have the resources to bring in professors or consultants for sessions with groups of executives, or even private one-on-one tutoring.

Understanding and Questioning Assumptions

We've already mentioned statistician George Box's famous quote, "All models are wrong, but some are useful." We mentioned at the time that it's important to know when they no longer become useful. That is generally when the assumptions built into the model—and all models have them—are no longer correct or valid. The world is always changing, and the job of the skeptical executive is to determine whether it has changed in ways that call the model into question. Here are some examples of assumptions in quantitative models that have actually been used by organizations:

- The customer's willingness to buy a product at a certain price (known as a price elasticity model) hasn't changed, even though the economy has deteriorated.

- The customer sample on which we tested various versions of Web pages several years ago is similar in their preferences to the customers we have today.

- The predictive model we created on mortgage holders' likelihood of default when housing prices were going up still holds when prices are declining (obviously, this one is somewhat problematic).

- The likelihood that a hurricane will hit a region of southern Florida hasn't gone up, even though we seem to be experiencing some degree of global climate change.

- A landline telephone number still provides a valid sample for a political poll, even though many people no longer have them (as we've suggested, this one is also problematic).

Not all of these assumptions were invalid. In fact, since almost all models are based on data from the past (remember, it's hard to get good data about the future), they make the assumption that the future is going to be like the past in most respects. And those models are very often valid for long periods of time. As Charles Duhigg has noted in a recent book, *The Power of Habit,* human behavior, once established, can be remarkably persistent over time.[4] That allows us to magically predict the future on the basis of the past.

Some organizations utilize high-priced talent just to ask penetrating questions about assumptions. Take Larry Summers, for example. The former economic adviser to the Clinton and Obama adminstrations and former president of Harvard University has worked as an adviser to D.E. Shaw, a quantitative hedge fund. Tom ran into Summers at a social occasion and asked him what he did for the company. He said, "I go in once a week and walk around the desks of the quants who build mathematical trading models. I ask them what the assumptions are behind their models, and under what circumstances they would be violated. You would be surprised how often they can't give me a clear answer." Summers was reportedly paid $5 million for playing this role, so it must have been perceived as valuable.

You too can act like Larry Summers. If someone presents you with a model, you can always look smart by asking what the assumptions are behind the model and what the conditions are that would invalidate them. If the reply is overly technical, keep pursuing the issue of how the world would have to change for the model to be no longer useful.

Push Back When You Don't Understand

The last point in the previous section can be generalized; it's important to push back when you don't understand. The most important form of pushing back is to request data and analysis, rather than anecdote or opinion. As Gary Loveman, CEO of Caesars Entertainment put it, "It is not my job to have all the answers, but it is my job to ask lots of penetrating, disturbing, and occasionally almost offensive questions as part of the analytic process that leads to insight and refinement."[5]

The specific types of questions that simply encourage greater use of analytics might go like this:

- "Did you forget your data?"

- "How do you think that hypothesis could be tested with data?"

- "Have you thought about an empirical analysis of that idea?"

- "We have about XX customers. Have you tried this out on any of them?"

- "Maybe you could consider a small but rigorous experiment on that concept."

You get the idea. If enough people around an organization constantly ask questions of this type, the culture will change quickly and dramatically.

Quantitative people will often attempt to describe models and problems in highly technical terms. That doesn't mean you have to listen or converse in the same terms. As a good illustration, the movie *Margin Call* dramatizes some of the events that led to the financial crisis of 2008–2009. The movie is based on an investment bank that resembles Lehman Brothers. The quant character in the plot, who has a PhD in propulsion engineering, comes up with a new algorithm for calculating the bank's exposure to risk. When he shows the algorithm to the head of trading, played by Kevin Spacey, the blustery trading czar says, "You know I can't read these things. Just speak to me in English."[6] Every manager should be similarly demanding.[7]

Liam Fahey, a marketing and strategy professor, has described in an article in *Strategy and Leadership* the roles of executives in making analytics work through a series of recommended questions.[8] They're a good summary of the topic of what to expect from executives. Here are the overall questions he recommends that executives ask:

- What business issue or need is the analytics work intended to inform?

- What are the core insights relevant to understanding the business issue and its context?

- How can I leverage these insights in the work I do?

- How do the insights affect decisions confronting us now?

- How do the insights help shape emerging and future decisions?

When preliminary findings begin to emerge, executives should ask:

- What is surprising about this finding?

- Can you do further analysis to strengthen or refute the finding?

- Should we get others involved to challenge this emerging finding?

- Is there a significant insight emerging here?

- If the finding holds up, how should it affect my thinking on this or other topics or issues?

For each new insight, executives should ask:

- What is new in each insight?

- What was the old understanding?

- How significant is the difference?

- What is the reasoning or "argument" that connects the data set to the insight?

After the insights have been delivered, executives should ask:

- Who was/is involved in shaping the new understanding?

- How might they have influenced the outcome?

- What might be the principal differences across individuals or units?

If you as an executive ask all these questions, you will be much more engaged in the analytical work, and the analysts will perceive you as being interested and knowledgeable. And if the analysts can answer them all clearly, they're doing a good job too!

What Should You Expect of Analytical Professionals?

Having spent some time describing the responsibilities of business decision makers in solving quantitative problems, it makes sense to also describe what analytical professionals need to do in order to meet the decision makers (more than) halfway. We've summarized these activities in "What Business Decision Makers Should Expect of Quantitative Analysts."

They Will Learn Your Business and Be Interested in Business Problems

Some quantitative analysts are primarily interested in quantitative methods and analysis itself, rather than the business problem to be solved. This is partly a function of our educational system, which tends to teach math and statistics in a relatively context-free format. But if quants don't focus on the business problem, they won't be able to solve it effectively or provide much value to decision makers.

The most important time to ensure that an analyst is interested in solving business problems is at the point of hiring and recruiting. Once he or she has been hired, it may be hard to bring about change. Anne Robinson, the head of an analytics group at Verizon Wireless, for example, asks any recruit to describe a specific business problem that he or she has addressed in the past, and what was interesting about it. Karl Kempf at Intel asks similar questions. If the recruit is stuck for an answer to that question—and both Robinson and Kempf report that many are, unfortunately—that person doesn't get hired.

They Will Talk in Business Terms

We've discussed this more than once throughout the book, and it's not an easy thing to do. But quantitative professionals need to learn how to translate their analysis approaches and findings into business

What Business Decision Makers Should Expect of Quantitative Analysts

If you're a business executive who is working with quantitative analysts, here's what you should legitimately expect of them:

• They should have a good working understanding of your business overall, and of the specific business process that the quantitative analysis will support.

• They should understand your thinking style and the types of analyses and outputs that will influence your thinking.

• They should be able to develop effective working relationships with key people in your organization.

• They should use the language of your business to explain what benefits and improvements analytics can provide.

• They should provide you with an accurate estimate of the time and cost to develop a model and related capabilities.

• If you don't understand what they're proposing to do, or you're skeptical of the benefits they predict, they should be patient and try again with different language.

• They should have a structured process for eliciting the information and business rules they need to build their model.

• They should help you think about such broad aspects of the problem as the framing of the decision involved, the stakeholders for it, and the organizational capabilities necessary to implement a new solution.

• Unless there is an important reason to do otherwise, new models and tool sets should be developed with a rapid prototyping approach, so you see something of substance very quickly and can provide feedback on it.

- They should iterate and improve the model until it meets your performance specifications.

- They should agree on a timeframe during which you will review the model, and explain to you what you should look for as signs that the model isn't working well and needs to be revisited.

terms. In many cases, that will mean using terminology with which business professionals are familiar—lift, ROI, customer behavior, money saved and earned. Talking about money all the time may strike some as a bit mercenary, but it is the language of business. In a government agency or nonprofit organization, there are usually translations that fit that context involving citizens, constituents, and budgets.

Patrick Moore, who heads a commercial analytics group at Merck (there is an example of his group's work at the end of the chapter), says that he tries to follow three rules of thumb when explaining analytical results in order to help his clients make better business decisions:

- Avoid the idea that the analysis is a "black box." That will make the client want to avoid it. So he tries to be very transparent.

- Convey the impression to business customers that the appropriate data has been looked at using appropriate methods; in other words, he and his analysts try to be and to appear confident that they have done the right thing analytically.

- Provide the client with "sound bites" or "thumbnails" of the results that they can use to turn around and communicate to their leadership.

Moore's group also makes extensive use of graphics displays to communicate, for example, the relative importance of different variables in a model. Even if clients don't fully understand the metric or statistic being used, they can grasp the relative importance of factors in a bar chart.

They Will Explain Any Technical Language

There may be times when quants will need to use some degree of technical language to explain what they have done. Even if that's true, quants should be ready with an explanation of what it means in English, and that means not being caught off guard. If there is a type of analytical tool or method that is used frequently, the quants in your organization may want to meet with colleagues and together determine a way to explain it in straightforward, clear wording. Of course, for relatively simple analyses—those involving a couple of variables—visual analytics are a powerful way to explain relationships within data.

They Are Willing to Develop a Relationship

As we mentioned earlier in this chapter, better decisions are not about the math, but about the relationships. If your quants don't want a relationship with businesspeople, perhaps they should go back to being an astrophysicist, forest ranger, or some other solitary profession, rather than being quantitative analysts in business.

This is easy to say, but it is true that many quants have historically preferred numbers to people. However, if you search for and interview for people-oriented quants and recruit at business-oriented analytics programs (such as the one at North Carolina State described in chapter 6), you can address this problem.

They Won't Make You Feel Stupid

We've seen a number of organizations in which quantitative people seemed to delight in making "normal" businesspeople feel stupid. They would say things like, "Surely you know what regression analysis is?" or, "I'm sorry, a chi-square test is just too elementary for me to have to explain." Some "heavy quants" (as one organization classified its more quantitatively sophisticated employees) even lorded it over the "light quants" in the same company.

Of course, this behavior is unacceptable and highly damaging to effective problem solving. However, like much bad behavior, we think it is often the result of people not feeling respected. In organizations where quants are intimately engaged in the business process and highly respected by decision makers, they tend to be wonderful people to work with. In organizations that somehow hired quantitative analysts but ignore them when important decisions come along, the nasty attitudes we've described often pop up. Quants, like most other people, respect others when they are respected.

Analytical Thinking Example: Demand Forecasting at Cisco

Forecasting customer demand is a problem for many firms, particularly in manufacturing.[9] It is a particularly important issue for Cisco Systems, the market-leading provider of telecommunications equipment. The company has a very complex global supply chain, and doesn't manufacture most of the products it sells. As Kevin Harrington, vice president of global business operations in Cisco's Customer

Value Chain Management organization put it: "Forecasting customer demand is, of course, a central part of supply chain management and a critical enabler of lean manufacturing. This discipline becomes ever more challenging in times like our own characterized by rapid changes in the macro-economy and volatile swings in supply and demand. In fact, Cisco's need to write off some unused inventory [\$2.25 billion worth] after the dotcom bust in 2001 provided some of the impetus for the larger transformation of our value chain."[10]

The resulting project is a good illustration not only of analytical thinking, but of good relationships between quantitative analysts and business decision makers.

PROBLEM RECOGNITION AND FRAMING. The problem for Cisco was simply to create a better forecast of demand across more than ten thousand different products. Managers in various parts of the company, including Sales, Marketing, and Finance, already created a "consensus forecast" using a combination of intuition and extrapolation of previous demand trends. But Karl Braitberg, Cisco's vice president of Demand Management and Planning, felt that a statistical forecast based on known booking and historical demand patterns would make a good "second opinion" for the human-derived consensus forecast, which can be affected by excessive marketing enthusiasm. He commissioned Anne Robinson, senior manager of Analytical Forecasting and Modeling, and her six-person team to try to develop a statistical forecast. Robinson realized that in order to be successful, she needed not only to create a high-quality forecast model, but also to get Cisco management to buy into and use the statistical forecasts. So she identified the key stakeholders for the model, and employed an "agile" model development process in which progressively capable outputs would be delivered at a regular frequency over the eighteen months of the project. At each output delivery step, she would show the results to stakeholders, educate them about the workings of the model, and—she hoped—get their buy-in for using it.

REVIEW OF PREVIOUS FINDINGS. There are a variety of approaches to statistical forecasting. Previous findings suggest that the best results are achieved through a combination of approaches to forecasting—an approach called *ensemble forecasting*. Robinson knew from her research and investigation that the ensemble approach offered potential, so she made sure that any forecasting tools her team explored had that capability.

MODELING (VARIABLE SELECTION). The key variables in the model would likely be current order levels and historical demand. These variables are commonly used in forecasting processes across industries.

DATA COLLECTION (MEASUREMENT). While the variables to be used were clear from the beginning, there were various diverse sources of current orders, and the different sources had to be evaluated to determine the data that was most valuable for the model. For example, Cisco tracks customer orders by industry segments, customer size segments, geographical area, and actual customer shipments. The data don't always add up perfectly. Fortunately, all the possible data sources were present in a preexisting enterprise data warehouse. However, Robinson's team also needed to create some new metrics of customer-centric demand fulfillment that became drivers of what it meant to be customer-centric throughout the Cisco supply chain.

DATA ANALYSIS. Statisical forecasting leads to a predicted range of demand, with a confidence interval for each range estimate. It might suggest, for example, that the monthly demand for a particular router would be between three thousand and thirty-five hundred units, with a 95 percent chance that the actual demand would be within that range. The "agile" approach to developing the model dictated a series of steps, each taking two to three months, to show that a successful model was possible and that it could scale to deal with the number and variability of Cisco's products. Some of the steps involved:

- Selecting a tool that fit the requirements (Cisco selected the SAS Forecast Server, which offers support for ensemble models)

- Determining whether statistical models could achieve better forecast accuracy than the consensus forecasts, and it did that

- Tuning the models to increase their accuracy

- Determining whether the forecasting approach could scale to thousands of products in three hundred product families (it could)

- Automating the models (it would be far too labor intensive for humans to run them, but Cisco managers and experts can still override them if necessary)

At each step, there was a stakeholder review, which built commitment to the new approach throughout the process.

RESULTS PRESENTATION AND ACTION. The statistical forecasting approach now produces weekly forecast ranges for more than eighteen thousand products over a twenty-four-month time horizon. Using the combination of the statistical and consensus forecasts, forecast accuracy has been improved by 12 percent on average. According to Kevin Harrington, the project was a success:

> The results include better forecast accuracy, increased inventory turns and an overall improvement in supply demand balancing that has paid off for both Cisco and our customers in the form of reduced excess inventory and faster, more reliable service. During the worst of the recent economic downturn, Cisco was able to reduce inventory in the supply chain without write-offs or a fall-off in customer service. Today, our statistical forecasting experts are working to further refine the entire process and manage the increased demand caused by the global economic recovery.[11]

In addition to the results that Harrington describes, Robinson notes that now managers at Cisco are comfortable with using ranges and probabilities to describe demand. They expect to see ranges rather than point (single number) forecasts, and talk about ranges in every important conversation. In short, the culture of forecasting at Cisco has changed dramatically in a more analytical direction.

Throughout the project, Robinson attempted to engage the entire forecasting community in the new analytical process. She went through a structured brainstorming process with stakeholders to help identify new customer-centric metrics. She had panel discussions with larger audiences, road shows for various groups, and a "Forecasting 101" presentation that she gave many times. She created visuals to display the results of the model, and encouraged her team to "tell a story with data" from the results. Robinson also built a close partnership with Cisco's IT organization, and she noted that at times it was difficult to distinguish between the tasks of her team and the tasks of IT people.

Analytical Thinking Example:
Optimizing the Sales Force at Merck

Identifying the ideal size for a sales force at a major pharmaceutical company like Merck is a difficult analytical task. New products are introduced regularly, increasing demand and the need for salespeople; existing products go off patent, which reduces demand and the need for salespeople. There is no history of demand for new products, so it's impossible to know just how to predict sales force needs exactly.

Many pharmaceutical companies employ external consultants for sales force sizing. However, when Paul Kallukaran, a quantitative PhD with experience in analyzing pharmaceutical sales data, joined the Commercial Analytics team, Merck executives decided to do the analysis in-house.

PROBLEM RECOGNITION AND FRAMING. With certain drugs coming off patent and other drugs entering the sales cycle, what should the optimal size of the sales force be? The sales force is not monolithic, but rather segmented by the brand and geography. So the problem was not to size the sales force overall, but rather to size it for each region and brand.

REVIEW OF PREVIOUS FINDINGS. Given that consulting firms offer sales force sizing services, there is some literature on it. Kallukaran's previous job was not directly in the area, but he had looked at approaches other firms had used. However, they tended to be "black box" oriented from the standpoint of sales and marketing decision makers, and Kallukaran and Patrick Moore, the head of Commercial Analytics, disliked that aspect. In the past, different groups at Merck had used different consultants and different methods for sales force sizing; this was the first time one central approach had been employed.

MODELING (VARIABLE SELECTION). Kallukaran decided to use multiple methods to determine the optimal sales force size. In addition to doing it the traditional way with statistical models, he and his team employed a more granular approach by trying to understand what it took to serve each customer. They asked the sales force about their activities with physician customers, and determined the likely workload for each one. They also computed various product forecasts and created nonlinear response models of sales force promotion and the likely change in physician prescribing as a result. They analyzed the impact of the sales force versus other factors that affect physician prescribing behaviors, including habit, brand equity, and pull by patients. The analysts also looked at patient-level data to understand adherence patterns over time; many patients exhibit significant drop-off in usage over time, which affects long-term sales of a drug. Finally, they employed an integer optimization model to optimize resources for each physician for each product for each of hundreds of territories.

DATA COLLECTION. The pharmaceuticals industry generally gets physician prescribing data from third-party syndicators, and Merck had that data. But the sales force activity model in the project required surveying salespeople on their sales behaviors and times with customers. They had to maintain the trust of the sales force—that is, survey them in a way that it didn't look like a downsizing exercise—so that salespeople wouldn't feel that their own jobs were threatened and would provide accurate answers.

DATA ANALYSIS. As we noted, the complex exercise involved a variety of analytical approaches, including integer optimization and nonparametric (not assuming a particular type of data distribution) models that computed response curves for each product segment on the basis of historical promotion responses. Since the project involved running models for each brand and territory, computing the whole model initially took sixteen hours. But Kallukaran's group wanted a faster response time, so they split the problem across hundreds of surplus laptop computers. Each laptop computed the model for a particular territory. With all that computing horsepower on tap, the entire model could be run in twenty minutes.

RESULTS PRESENTATION AND ACTION. While this was a new approach to the sales force sizing problem at Merck, it was not entirely unfamiliar to internal clients—which made it easier to get them to adopt the model and act on the results. On the sales side, the VP of Strategic Planning had an analytical orientation, and exposure to what consultants had done in this area in the past. On the marketing side, analysts had previously done models of promotion response, but they didn't get used. Someone always complained that the model lacked this piece or that; the perfect had become the enemy of the good. With the sales force sizing project, Kallukaran encouraged the marketing clients to "use what we have." He initially worked with one of the smaller brand teams first and showed why the new approach was better than the more intuitive decision approach they were using before. He contrasted that intuitive method with what data and analytics would tell them, but didn't try to impose the model-based approach on them. "Take it as just another input to your decision," he would say. The efforts to persuade different groups to use the model were aided by the consistent approach across the company. Merck's president at the time liked the idea of being able to compare different brand team needs so that he could more easily evaluate their requests for resources. Over time, almost all groups at Merck adopted the model. Kallukaran's analytics team also was getting requests to recompute the model whenever there was a vacancy in a particular territory, and territory managers had been given more autonomy and profit-and-loss responsibility. So the team, which included system developers, created an "analytical app" that tells a sales manager whether to fill a vacancy or not. It has been widely used and allows local decision making without putting heavy demands on Kallukaran's central group.

Final Thoughts on Analytical Thinking

By this point—effectively the end of the book unless you really enjoy perusing footnotes—we hope to have convinced you of a number of things. First, that analytical thinking and decisions based on data and analytics will play an increasingly important role in business and society. We'll need many managers and professionals who are comfortable with analytical thinking, and we want you to be one of those. Second, we hope you now realize that you can play in this game even if you are not a statistics or math whiz. If you understand the stages and steps of analytical thinking and the attributes of a good analytical decision process, you can engage with the best quants and help to improve the outcome. You'll also make yourself a better thinker and decision maker along the way.

Third, while most people typically think of "solving the problem" as the core of analytical thinking, it's only one of the steps that make for a successful analytical decision. If the problem is framed incorrectly or sub-optimally, the solution won't be very useful. And if the results aren't communicated in an effective way, it's unlikely that any decision will be made on the basis of them, or any actions taken. If you're working on an analytical problem and trying to think of how to allocate your time, start with an equal allocation across these three stages.

Fourth and finally, many people believe that the world of analytical thinking and decisions is almost exclusively about numbers, rigorous statistics, and left-brain thinking in general. But the right brain needs to be seriously engaged as well. We've tried to show—in chapter 5 especially—that creativity is important to analytical thinking, and in this chapter have argued (based on lots of experience and observation) that relationships are just as important—perhaps more so—to progress with analytics than sheer number-crunching ability.

If you have read this entire book and given the ideas and examples some thought, you are now prepared to join the ranks of analytical thinkers. Congratulations! It's an exciting time to be in this group. The amount and importance of data in organizations is only going to shoot upward over time, and you will be able to move upward with it. We expect that your newfound analytical focus will benefit both your career and the success of the organizations you work with.

Notes

Chapter 1

1. Xiao-Li Meng, abstract, "Statistical Education and Educating Statisticians: Producing Wine Connoisseurs and Master Winemakers," seminar presented at the University of Minnesota, October 28, 2011, http://catalystsumn.blogspot.com/2011/11/statistics-education-seminar-presented.html.

2. "Big Data: The Next Frontier for Innovation, Competition, and Productivity," McKinsey Global Institute, May 2011, http://www.mckinsey.com/insights/mgi/research/technology_and_innovation/big_data_the_next_frontier_for_innovation.

3. R. M. Dawes, D. Faust, and P. E. Meehl, "Clinical Versus Actuarial Judgment," *Science* 243, no. 4899 (March 1989): 1668–1674.

Chapter 2

1. S. Babou, "What Is Stakeholder Analysis?" The Project Management Hut, http://www.pmhut.com/what-is-stakeholder-analysis.

2. "Expedia Travels to New Heights," *SASCom Magazine,* Third Quarter 2011, 14.

3. All of these testing stories are examples from customers of Applied Predictive Technologies, a software company, though we approached the companies independently. For more on the methods behind this approach, see Thomas H. Davenport, "How to Design Smart Business Experiments," *Harvard Business Review,* November 2009.

4. Mireya Navarro, "For Many Latinos, Race Is More Culture Than Color," *New York Times,* January 13, 2012.

5. W.A. Wallis and H.V. Roberts, *Statistics: A New Approach* (New York: Free Press, 1960).

6. Lisa Carley-Baxter et al., "Comparison of Cell Phone and Landline Surveys: A Design Perspective," *Field Methods* 22, no. 1 (February 2010): 3–15.

7. Saul Hansell, "Google Answer to Filling Jobs Is an Algorithm," *New York Times,* January 3, 2007, www.nytimes.com/2007/01/03/technology/03google.html.

8. "Joseph Jagger," Wikipedia, http://en.wikipedia.org/wiki/Joseph_Jagger; "Joseph Jagger: The Man Who Broke the Bank," www.wildjackcasino.com/

joseph-jagger.html; "Joseph Jagger," www.realmoneycasinos.net/joseph-jagger.html; "Roulette—The Men Who Broke the Bank at Monte Carlo—Joseph Jagger," www.wiseguyroulette.com/roulette-history/joseph-jagger/.

9. Rama Ramakrishnan, "Three Ways to Analytic Impact," *The Analytic Age* blog, July 26, 2011, http://blog.ramakrishnan.com/.

10. *People v. Collins,* 68 Cal. 2d 319 (1968); http://scholar.google.com/scholar_case?case=2393563144534950884; "*People v. Collins,*" http://en.wikipedia.org/wiki/People_v._Collins.

Chapter 3

1. A. M. Starfield, Karl A. Smith, and A. L. Bleloch, *How to Model It: Problem Solving for the Computer Age* (New York: McGraw-Hill, 1994), 19.

2. George Box and Norman R. Draper, *Empirical Model-Building and Response Surfaces* (New York: Wiley, 1987), 424.

3. Garth Sundem, *Geek Logik: 50 Foolproof Equations for Everyday Life,* (New York: Workman, 2006).

4. Minnie Brashears, *Mark Twain, Son of Missouri* (Whitefish, MT: Kessinger Publishing, 2007).

5. Ernest E. Leisy, ed., *The Letters of Quintus Curtius Snodgrass* (Irving, TX: University Press of Dallas, 1946).

6. Claude S. Brinegar, "Mark Twain and the Quintus Curtius Snodgrass Letters: A Statistical Test of Authorship," *Journal of the American Statistical Association* 58 (1963).

7. R. C. Rosen et. al., "The International Index of Erectile Function (IIFF): A Multidimensional Scale for Assessment of Erectile Function," *Urology* 49, no, 6 (1997): 822–830. R. C. Rosen et. al., "Development and Evaluation of an Abridged, 5-item Version of the International Index of Erectile Function (IIEF-5) as a Diagnostic Tool for Erectile Dysfunction," *International Journal of Impotence Research* 11 (1999): 319–326.

8. Rama Ramakrishnan, "Three Ways to Analytic Impact," *The Analytic Age* (blog), July 26, 2011, http://blog.ramakrishnan.com/.

9. Anand Rajaraman, "More Data Usually Beats Better Algorithms," *Datawocky* (blog), March 24, 2008, http://anand.typepad.com/datawocky/2008/03/more-data-usual.html.

10. Daryl Morey, "Success Comes from Better Data, Not Better Analysis," blog post, *Harvard Business Review,* August 8, 2011, http://blogs.hbr.org/cs/2011/08/success_comes_from_better_data.html.

11. "Tycho Brahe," *Wikipedia,* http://en.wikipedia.org/wiki/Tycho_Brahe; Michael Fowler, "Tycho Brahe," http://galileoandeinstein.physics.virginia.edu/1995/lectures/tychob.html; Arthur Koestler, *The Watershed: A Biography of Johannes Kepler* (Doubleday, 1960); "Johannes Kepler," *Wikipedia,* http://en.wikipedia.org/wiki/Johannes_Kepler; "Johannes Kepler: The Laws of Planetary Motion," http://csep10.phys.utk.edu/astr161/lect/history/kepler.html; Michael Fowler, "Tycho Brahe and Johannes Kepler," http://galileoandeinstein.physics.virginia.edu/lectures/tycho.htm; Michael Fowler, "Johannes Kepler," http://galileoandeinstein.physics.virginia.edu/1995/lectures/kepler.html; "Johannes Kepler," *Encyclopædia Britannica Online Academic Edition,* http://www.britannica.com/EBchecked/topic/315225/Johannes-Kepler; Ann Lamont, "Johannes Kepler: Outstanding Scientist and Committed Christian," *1:1,* http://www.answersingenesis.org/creation/v15/i1/kepler.asp, December 1, 1992.

12. Bill Franks, "Why Nobody Is Actually Analyzing Unstructured Data," International Institute for Analytics blog post, March 9, 2012, http://iianalytics.com/2012/03/why-nobody-is-actually-analyzing-unstructured-data/.

13. Peter Passell, "Wine Equation Puts Some Noses Out of Joint," *New York Times*, March 4, 1990.

14. "Alternative Rich List," FT.com, September 22, 2006.

15. Fischer Black and Myron Scholes, "The Pricing of Options and Corporate Liabilities," *Journal of Political Economy* 81, no. 3 (1973): 637–654; "Black–Scholes," *Wikipedia,* http://en.wikipedia.org/wiki/Black–Scholes; "The Prize in Economics 1997," press release, Nobelprize.org, http://nobelprize.org/nobel_prizes/economics/laureates/1997/press.html.

16. Fischer Black and Myron Scholes, "The Pricing of Options and Corporate Liabilities," *Journal of Political Economy* 81, no. 3 (May 1973).

17. R. J. Larsen and M. L. Marx, *An Introduction to Mathematics Statistics and Its Applications* (Englewood Cliffs, NJ: Prentice-Hall, 1981), 159. The particular column cited has been reprinted in many statistics textbooks and courses.

Chapter 4

1. Xiao-Li Meng, abstract, "Statistical Education and Educating Statisticians: Producing Wine Connoisseurs and Master Winemakers," seminar presented at the University of Minnesota, October 28, 2011, http://catalystsumn.blogspot.com/2011/11/statistics-education-seminar-presented.html.

2. Xiao-Li Meng, "Statistics: Your Chance for Happiness (or Misery)," course description, http://www.stat.harvard.edu/Academics/invitation_chair_txt.html.

3. David Schmitt, "Tell a Story," June 27, 2012, http://www.allanalytics.com/author.asp?id=2092&doc_id=246428.

4. I. Bernard Cohen, *The Triumph of Numbers: How Counting Shaped Modern Life* (New York: W.W. Norton, 2006), chapter 9; "Florence Nightingale," *Wikipedia,* http://en.wikipedia.org/wiki/Florence_Nightingale; P. Nuttall, "The Passionate Statistician," *Nursing Times* 28 (1983): 25–27.

5. Gregor Mendel, "Experiments in Plant Hybridization," http://www.mendelweb.org/; "Gregor Mendel," *Wikipedia,* http://en.wikipedia.org/wiki/Gregor_Mendel; Seung Yon Rhee, Gregor Mendel, *Access Excellence,* http://www.accessexcellence.org/RC/AB/BC/Gregor_Mendel.php; "Mendel's Genetics," anthro.palomar.edu/mendel/mendel_1.htm; David Paterson, "Gregor Mendel," www.zephyrus.co.uk/gregormendel.html; "Rocky Road: Gregor Mendel," *Strange Science,* www.strangescience.net/mendel.htm; Wolf-Ekkehard Lönnig, "Johann Gregor Mendel: Why His Discoveries Were Ignored for 35 Years," www.weloennig.de/mendel02.htm; "Gregor Mendel and the Scientific Milieu of His Discovery," www.2iceshs.cyfronet.pl/2ICESHS_Proceedings/Chapter_10/R-2_Sekerak.pdf; "Mendelian Inheritance," *Wikipedia,* http://en.wikipedia.org/wiki/Mendelian_inheritance.

6. This list was adapted and modified from one on the IBM ManyEyes site; see http://www-958.ibm.com/software/data/cognos/manyeyes/page/Visualization_Options.html.

7. This example is from the SAS Visual Analytics 5.1 User's Guide, "Working with Automatic Charts," http://support.sas.com/documentation/cdl/en/vaug/65384/HTML/default/viewer.htm#n1xa25dv4fiyz6n1etsfkbz75ai0.htm.

8. Hans Rosling, "Stats That Reshape Your Worldview," TED talk, February 2006, http://www.ted.com/talks/hans_rosling_shows_the_best_stats_you_ve_ever_seen.html.

9. While Schmitt's group sometimes creates such videos in-house, this one was done by an external production company.

10. James Taylor, "Decision Management Systems: A Practical Guide to Using Business Rules and Predictive Analytics," IBM Press, 2011.

11. Thomas H. Davenport, "How Companies Make Better Decisions," International Institute of Analytics, 2010, www.sas.com/decisions.

12. Ch'ananda, S. (1990), "The Origin of Go," *British Go Journal,* 79, Spring, 18-19.

13. Jinho Kim and Hyung Jun Kim, "The Advantage of Playing First in Go," *CHANCE* 8, no. 3 (1995): 22–26.

14. Interview with Gottman in http://www.edge.org/3rd_culture/gottman05/gottman05_index.html.

15. FICO score information comes from: "FICO Credit Score Chart," www.myfico.com/crediteducation/whatsinyourscore.aspx; "Credit Score in the United States," *Wikipedia,* http://en.wikipedia.org/wiki/Credit_score_in_the_United_States; Malgorzata Wozniacka and Snigdha Sen, "Credit Scores: What You Should Know About Your Own," *PBS Frontline,* November 2004, http://www.pbs.org/wgbh/pages/frontline/shows/credit/more/scores.html.

Chapter 5

1. Adam Satariano and Peter Burrows, "Apple's Supply Chain Secret? Hoard Lasers," *Bloomberg BusinessWeek,* November 03, 2011, http://www.businessweek.com/magazine/apples-supplychain-secret-hoard-lasers-11032011.html.

2. Online job description at: http://jobs.apple.com/index.ajs?BID=1&method=mExternal.showJob&RID=81197, accessed January 5, 2012.

3. Darrell Huff, *How to Lie with Statistics* (New York: Norton, 1954).

4. Junxiang Lu, "Predicting Customer Churn in the Telecommunications Industry: An Application of Survival Analysis Modeling Using SAS," SAS User Group International Proceedings, 2002.

5. Tim Drye, Graham Wetherill, and Alison Pinnock,"When Are Customers in the Market? Applying Survival Analysis to Marketing Challenges," *Journal of Targeting, Measurement and Analysis for Marketing* 10 (2001): 179–188.

6. Joel M. Hektner, Jennifer A. Schmidt, Mihaly Csikszentmihalyi, *Experience Sampling Method: Measuring the Quality of Everyday Life* (Thousand Oaks, CA: Sage, 2007).

7. Mihaly Csikszentmihalyi and Reed Larson, *Being Adolescent: Conflict and Growth in the Teenage Years* (New York: Basic Books, 1984).

8. "Archimedes," *Wikipedia,* http://en.wikipedia.org/wiki/Archimedes; "Eureka," *Wikipedia,* http://en.wikipedia.org/wiki/Eureka; Rohini Chowdhury, "'Eureka!': The Story of Archimedes and the Golden Crown," *Long, Long Time Ago,* http://www.longlongtimeago.com/llta_greatdiscoveries_archimedes_eureka.html; John Monahan, "Archimedes Coins 'Eureka!' in the Nude—and Other Crazy Ah-Ha Moments of Science," *Scientific American,* December 7, 2010, http://www.scientificamerican.com/article.cfm?id=archimedes-coins-eurekaeureka.

9. Robert and Michèle Root-Bernstein, *Sparks of Genius: The Thirteen Thinking Tools of the World's Most Creative People* (Boston: Houghton Mifflin, 1999), 4.

10. Cho Jung Rae, *The Enchanted Prison of Writing* (Seoul: Sisain Books, 2009), 394.

11. Hegel's ideas are, of course, complex and difficult to summarize. A deep discussion of these concepts can be found in Tom Rockmore, *Hegel, Idealism, and Analytic Philosophy* (New Haven: Yale University Press, 2005).

12. There are many versions of this story, but the most definitive account comes from Dan Power's DSS News, November 10, 2002, http://dssresources.com/newsletters/66.php.

13. John Earle, quoted in Riggs Eckleberry's "Of Interest" (blog), December 21, 1998, http://www.riggs.com/archives/1998_12_01_OIarchive.html.

14. David Snowdon et. al., "Linguistic Ability in Early Life and Cognitive Function and Alzheimer's Disease in Late Life," *JAMA,* 275 (1996): 528–532. "Landmark Study Links Cognitive Ability of Youth with Alzheimer's," http://archive.hhs.gov/news/press/1996pres/960220b.html.

15. Snowdon, et. al., "Linguistic Ability in Early Life."

16. Jodith Janes, review of David Snowdon's *Aging with Grace, Library Journal* 126, no. 11 (June 2001): 96.

17. Tiffany Sharples, "Can Language Skills Ward Off Alzheimer's? A Nuns' Study," *Time,* July 09, 2009, http://www.time.com/time/health/article/0,8599,1909420,00.html#ixzz1p7bYUKSu.

18. Email correspondence with Anthony Viel, November 9, 2011.

Chapter 6

1. Derrick Niederman and David Boyum, *What the Numbers Say: A Field Guide to Mastering Our Numerical World* (New York: Broadway Books, 2003), 233.

2. Linda Rosa, Emily Rosa, and Larry Sarner, "A Close Look at Therapeutic Touch," *Journal of American Medical Association* 279, no. 13 (1998): 1005–1010; Douglas W. Hubbard, *How To Measure Anything* (Hoboken, NJ: Wiley, 2010), 13–17.

3. Kevin Courcey, "Therapeutic Touch: Further Notes," www.quackwatch.org/01QuackeryRelatedTopics/tt2.html.

4. From "The Phenom List—The Top Big Data Scientists: DJ Patil," http://thephenomlist.com/Big_Data_Scientists/DJ_Patil, accessed February 23, 2012. Other information from interviews with Patil.

5. Darrell Huff, *How to Lie with Statistics* (New York: Norton, 1954).

6. Stephen K. Campbell, *Flaws and Fallacies in Statistical Thinking* (Englewood Cliffs, NJ: Prentice-Hall, 1974).

7. Phillip I. Good and James W. Hardin, *Common Errors in Statistics* (New York: Wiley, 2003).

8. Nassim Nicholas Taleb, *Fooled by Randomness: The Hidden Role of Chance in Life and the Markets* (New York: Random House, 2005).

9. Richard Isaac, *The Pleasures of Probability* (New York: Springer, 1995).

10. Leonard Mlodinow, *The Drunkard's Walk: How Randomness Rules Our Lives* (New York: Pantheon, 2008).

11. See http://ocw.mit.edu/courses/mathematics/18-05-introduction-to-probability-and-statistics-spring-2005/.

12. Information on the NC State MSA from several meetings with program administrators and faculty, and from "Institute for Advanced Analytics, North Carolina State University," analytics.ncsu.edu.

13. These preliminary figures from the "State of Business Intelligence in Academia 2011" report were presented by Barbara Wixom at the Third BI Congress, Orlando, FL, December 16, 2012.

14. Quoted in Thomas Dietz and Linda Kalof, *Introduction to Social Statistics: The Logic of Statistical Reasoning* (New York: Wiley, 2009), xxviii.

15. Campbell, *Flaws and Fallacies in Statistical Thinking,* 108.

16. Christopher Chabris and Daniel Simons, *The Invisible Gorilla and Other Ways Our Intuitions Deceives Us* (New York: Crown, 2010), 163.

17. Heinz Kohler, *Statistics for Business and Economics* (London: Longman, 1988).

18. Amazon review from "A 'Umea University' student (Sweden) give ratings," August 24, 1999, http://www.amazon.com/review/R2LQ3TGC1PC51D/ref=cm_cr_dp_title?ie=UTF8&ASIN=0673184447&channel=detail-glance&nodeID=283155&store=books, retrieved December 30, 2012.

19. Michael Lewis, *Moneyball: The Art of Winning an Unfair Game* (New York: Norton, 2003).

20. "SN Names the 20 Smartest Athletes in Sports," *The Sporting News*, Sept. 23, 2010, http://aol.sportingnews.com/mlb/feed/2010-09/smart-athletes/story/sporting-news-names-the-20-smartest-athletes-in-sports.

21. Michael Lewis, "The No-Stats All Star," *New York Times*, February 13, 2009, www.nytimes.com/2009/02/15/magazine/15Battier-t.html.

22. Frances X. Frei and Mathew Perlberg, "Discovering Hidden Gems: The Story of Daryl Morey, Shane Battier, and the Houston Rockets (B)," Harvard Business School case study (Boston: Harvard Business Publishing, September 2010), 1.

Chapter 7

1. Personal communication with author.

2. "Surveying the Economic Horizon: A Conversation with Robert Shiller," *McKinsey Quarterly*, April 2009, http://www.mckinseyquarterly.com/Surveying_the_economic_horizon_A_conversation_with_Robert_Shiller_2345.

3. David Olive, "Getting Wise Before That 'One Big Mistake,'" *Toronto Star*, December 17, 2007.

4. Charles Duhigg, *The Power of Habit: Why We Do What We Do in Life and Business* (New York: Random House, 2012).

5. Gary Loveman, "Foreword," in Thomas H. Davenport and Jeanne G. Harris, *Competing on Analytics: The New Science of Winning* (Boston: Harvard Business School Press, 2007), x.

6. More context on the movie and the characters can be found at http://business-ethics.com/2011/11/23/0953-margin-call-a-small-movie-unveils-big-truths-about-wall-street/.

7. *Margin Call*, film with direction and screenplay by J. C. Chandor, 2011.

8. Liam Fahey, "Exploring 'Analytics' to Make Better Decisions: The Questions Executives Need to Ask," *Strategy and Leadership* 37, no. 5 (2009): 12–18.

9. Information for this example came from several interviews with Anne Robinson; and Blake Johnson, "Leveraging Enterprise Data and Advanced Analytics in Core Operational Processes: Demand Forecasting at Cisco," case study, Stanford University Management Science and Engineering Department.

10. Kevin Harrington, "Seeing the Future in Value Chain Management," *Analytics Magazine*, March/April 2010.

11. Ibid.

Index

About the Authors

THOMAS H. DAVENPORT is a visiting professor at Harvard Business School, the President's Distinguished Professor of IT and Management at Babson College, and a research fellow at the MIT Center for Digital Business. He is also a senior advisor to Deloitte Analytics and the cofounder and research director of the International Institute for Analytics. Davenport is the coauthor of *Competing on Analytics* and *Analytics at Work*. This is the seventeenth book he has authored, coauthored, or edited.

JINHO KIM is a professor of business and statistics at the Korea National Defense University and the research director of the KNDU Lab for Analytics Research. He holds a PhD from the Wharton School and is the author of six books published in Korea, including the best-selling *100 Common Senses in Statistics* and *Freak Statistics*. He has developed and run an educational program for building individuals' analytical skills. His current research focuses on the use of analytical methods to address various issues in business and society.